Pearls of Wisdom

The Southern Sass of Nancy Parsons

**As featured in
The Haunting on Palm Court:
An Isle of Palms Suspense.**

Stephanie Edwards

Dear coloring book enthusiast,

It's my pleasure to share sassy Southernisms by Nancy Parsons, a character from The Haunting on Palm Court: An Isle of Palms Suspense.

I've always lived in the South. Nancy was inspired by the many women who have shaped my life. I hope this coloring book brings you some laughs and a glimpse into Southern life.

Now, y'all don't be strangers, ya hear? I hope to see you on Palm Court and social media, of course!

Stephanie Edwards

Author of The Haunting on Palm Court

Find me on:

 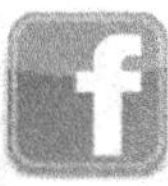 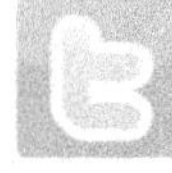

www.stephedwardswrites.com

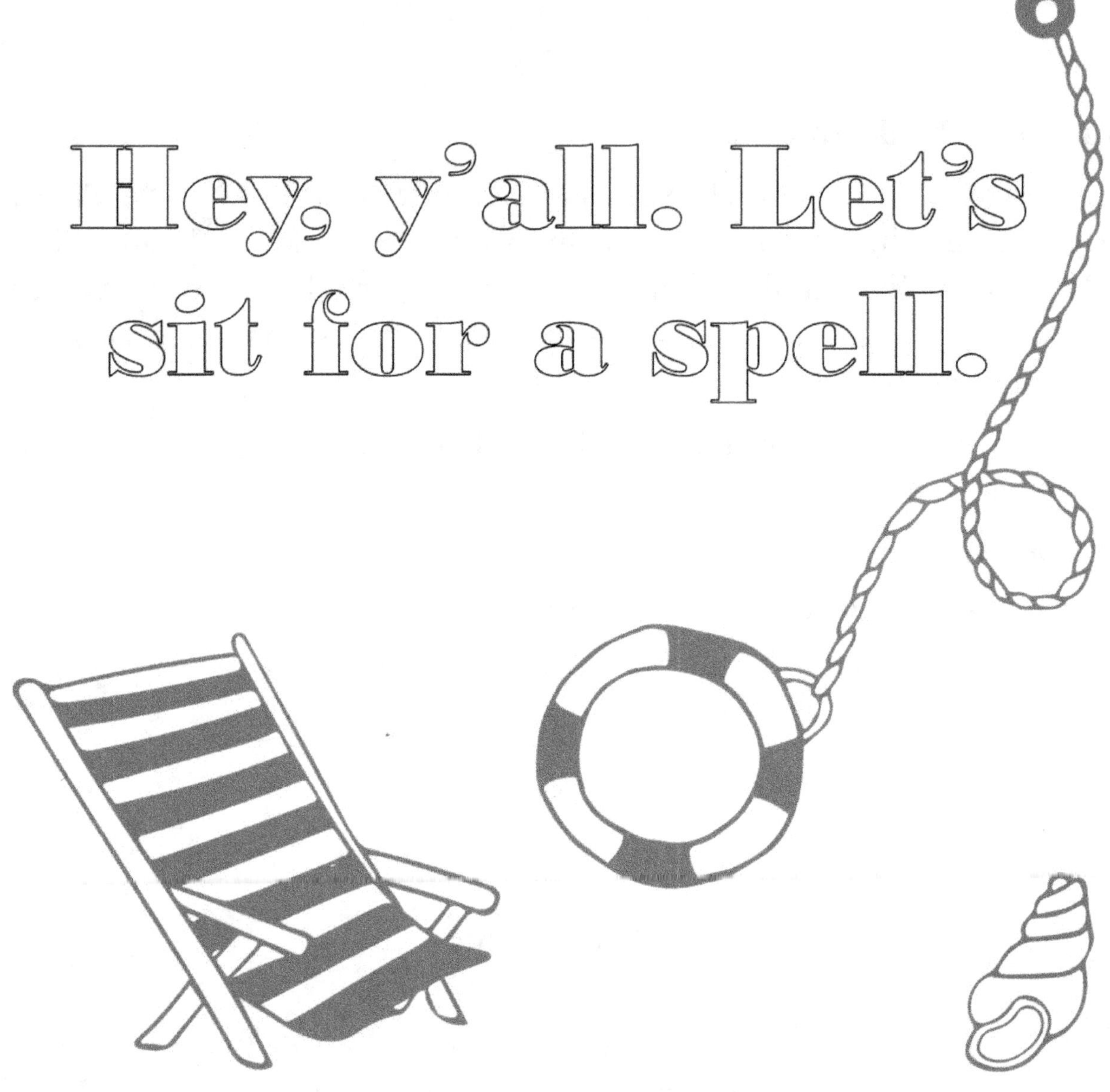
Hey, y'all. Let's sit for a spell.

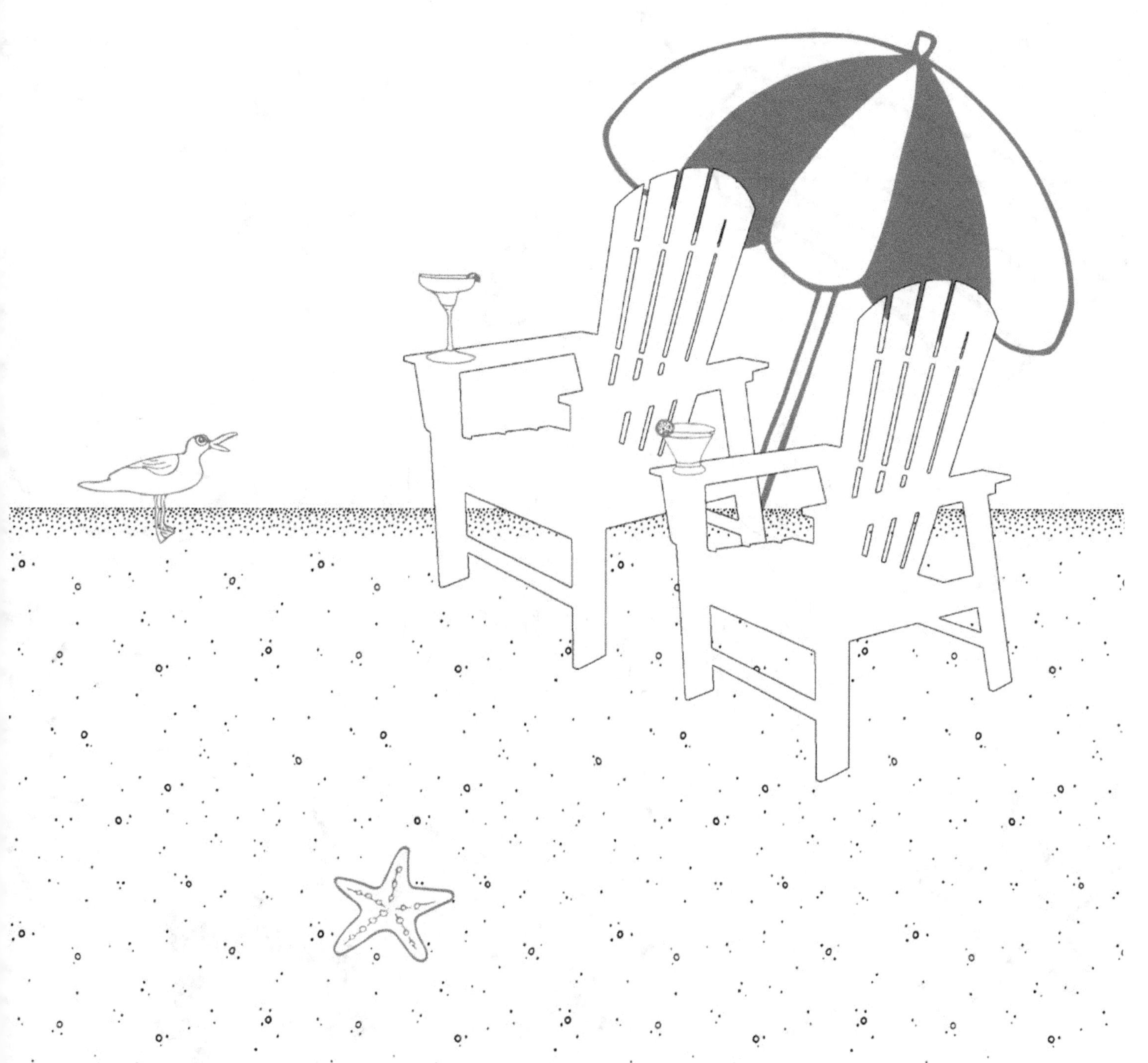

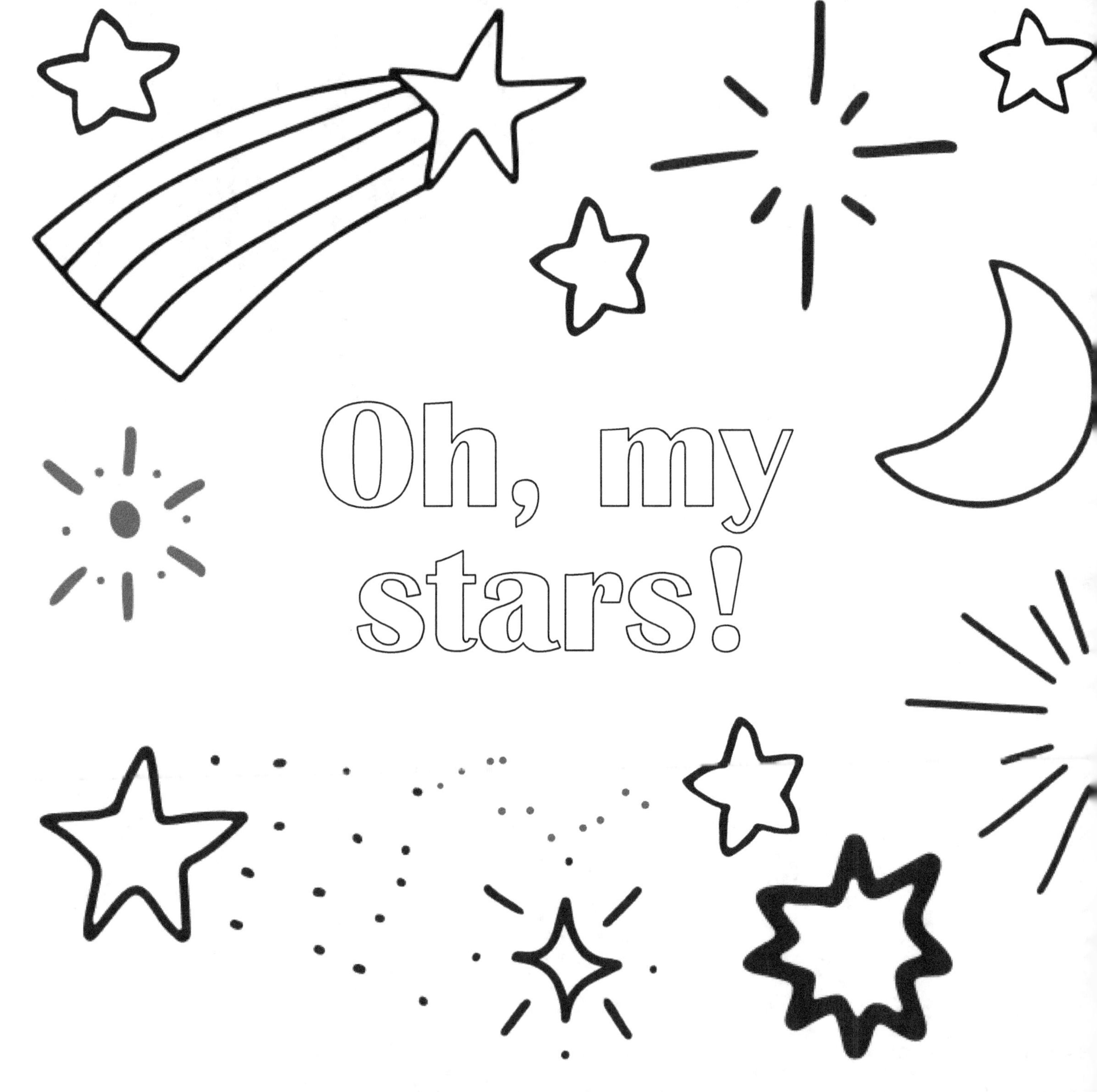

Oh, my
stars!

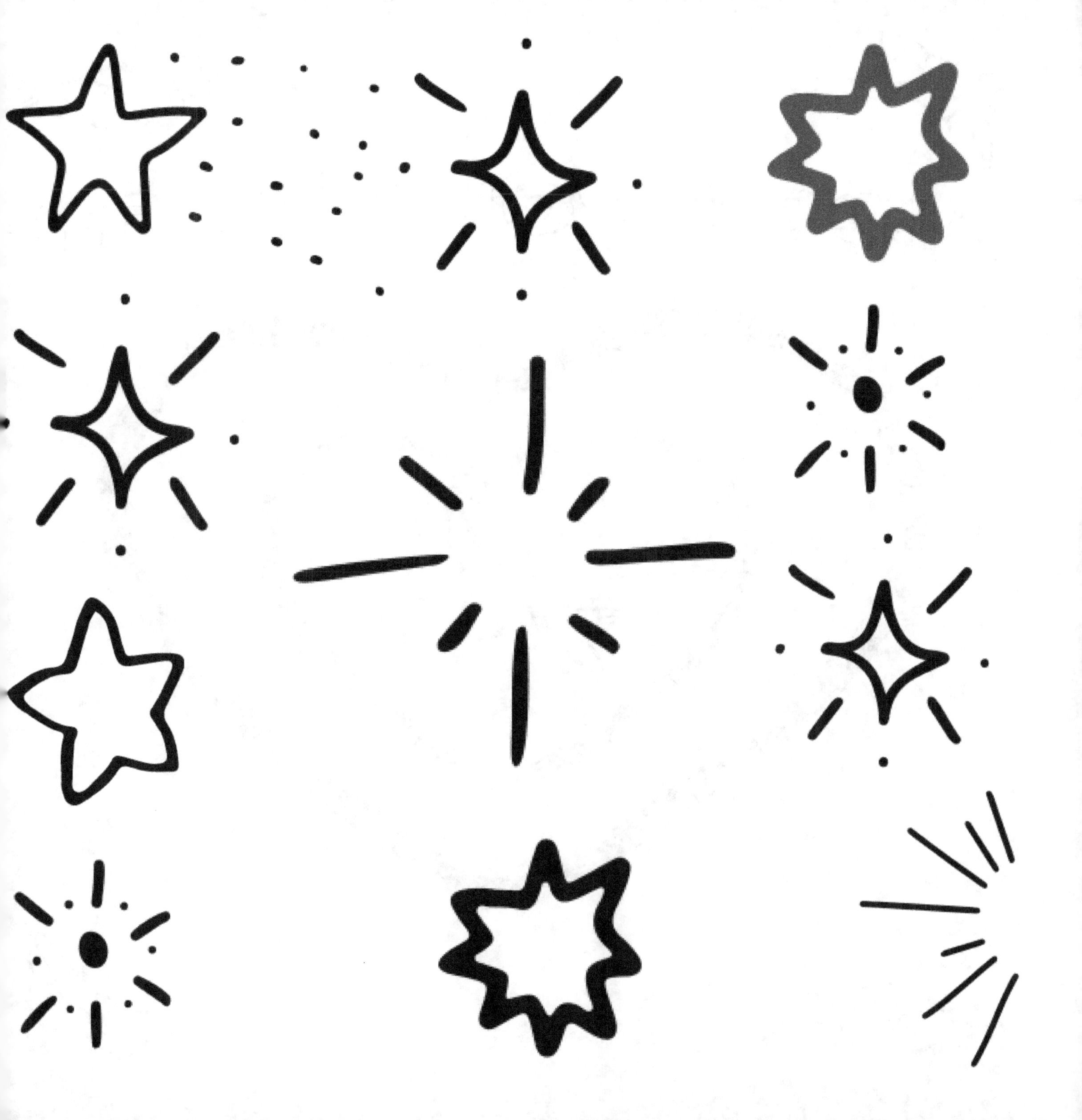

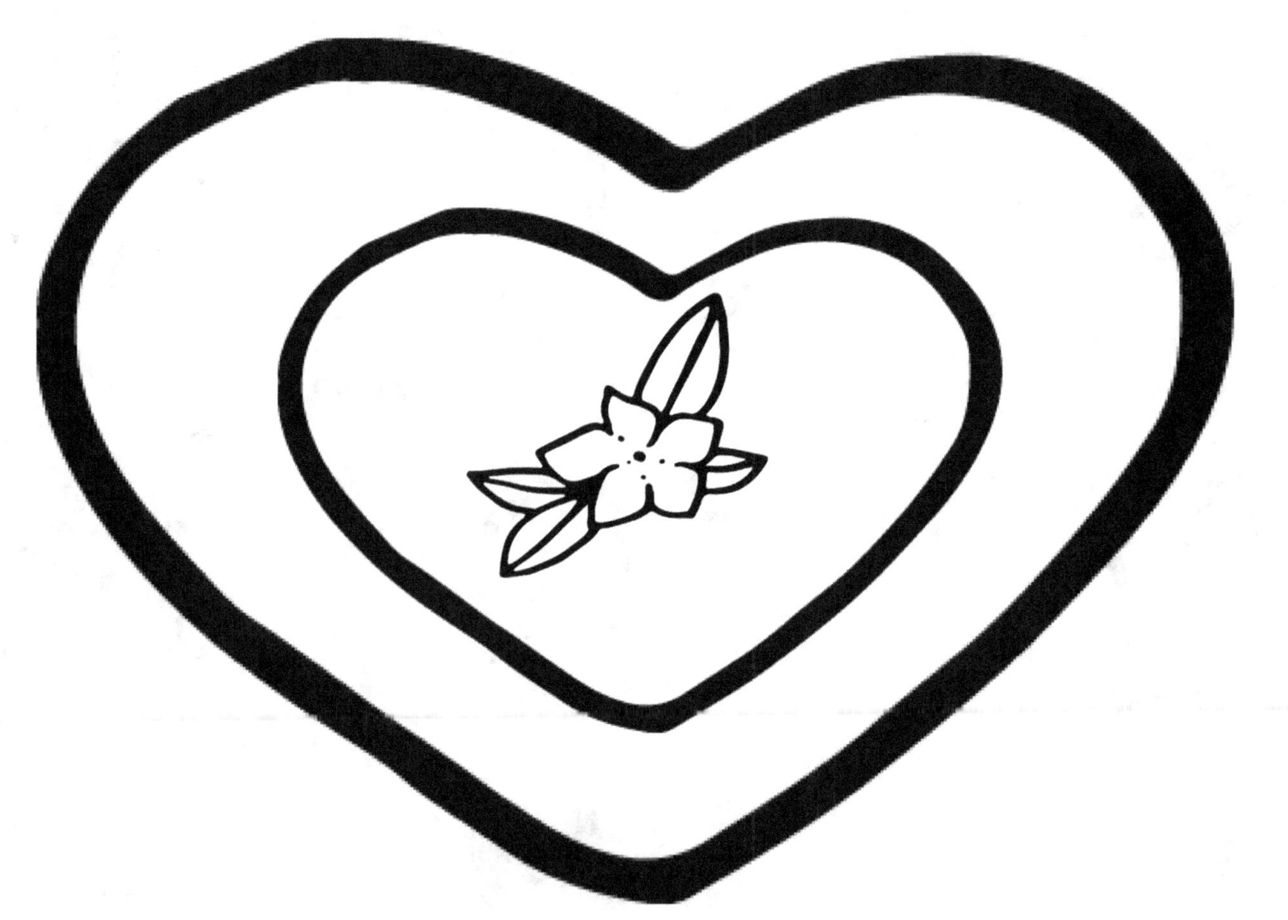

Bless your heart

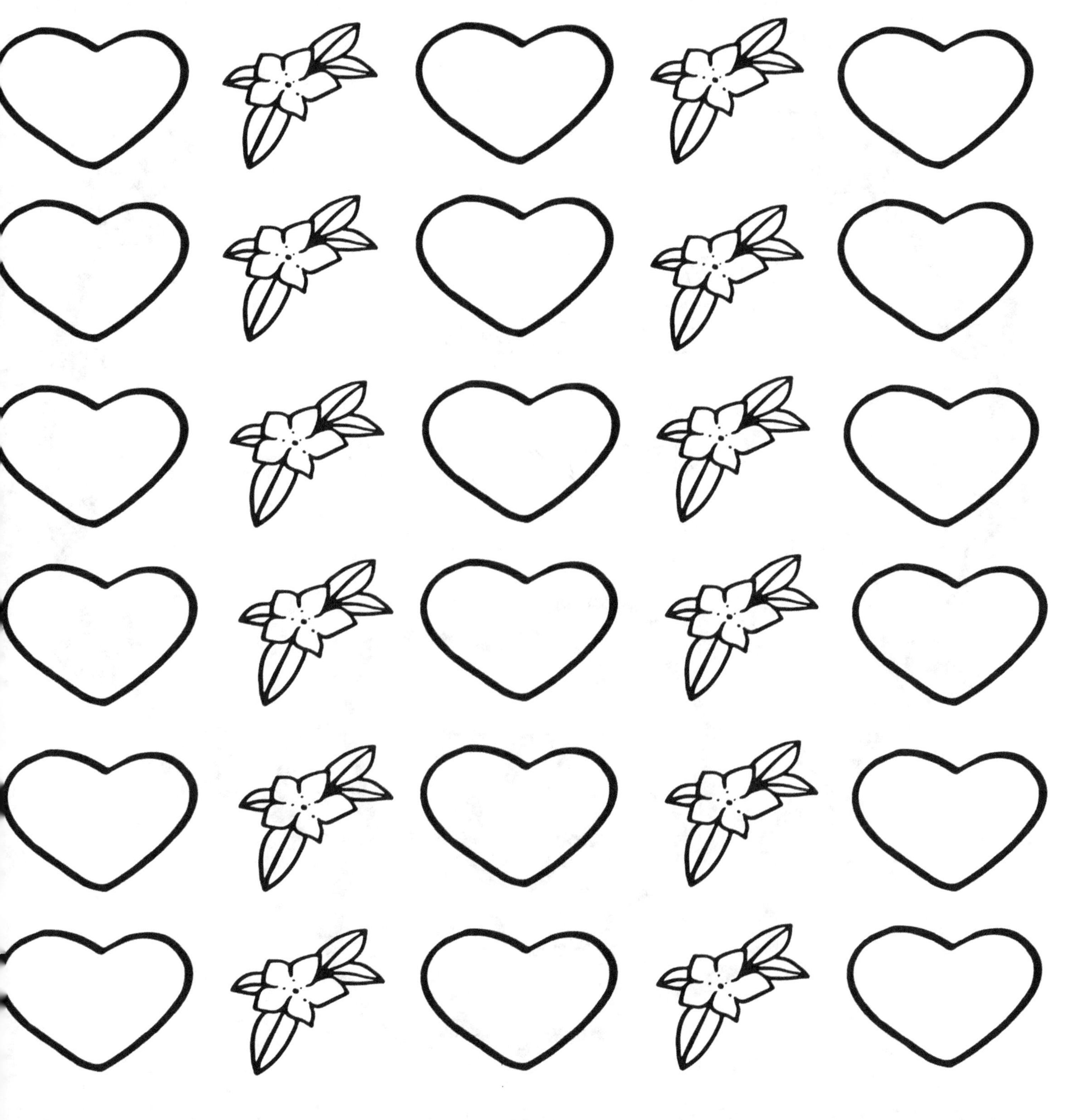

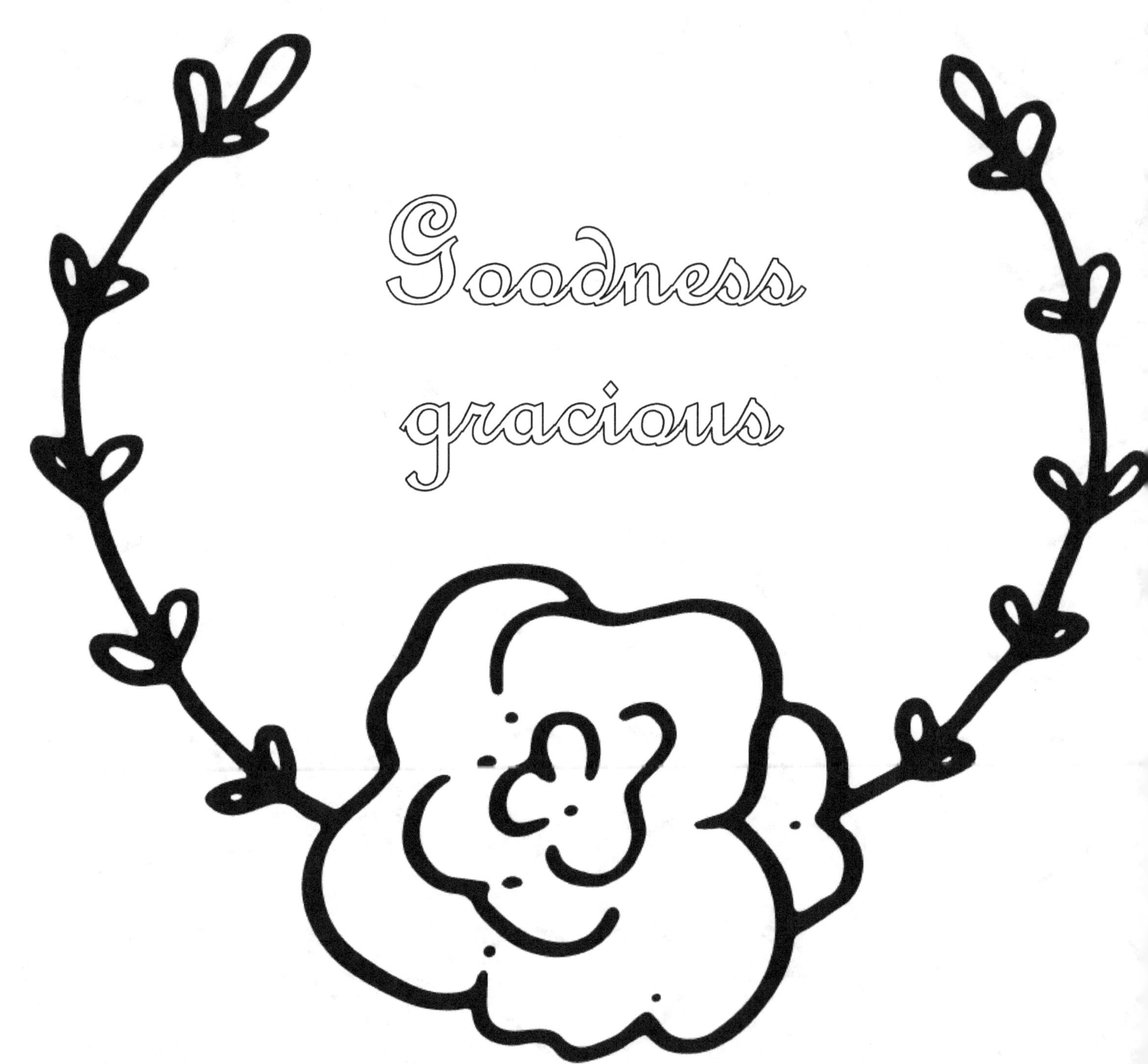

Goodness
gracious

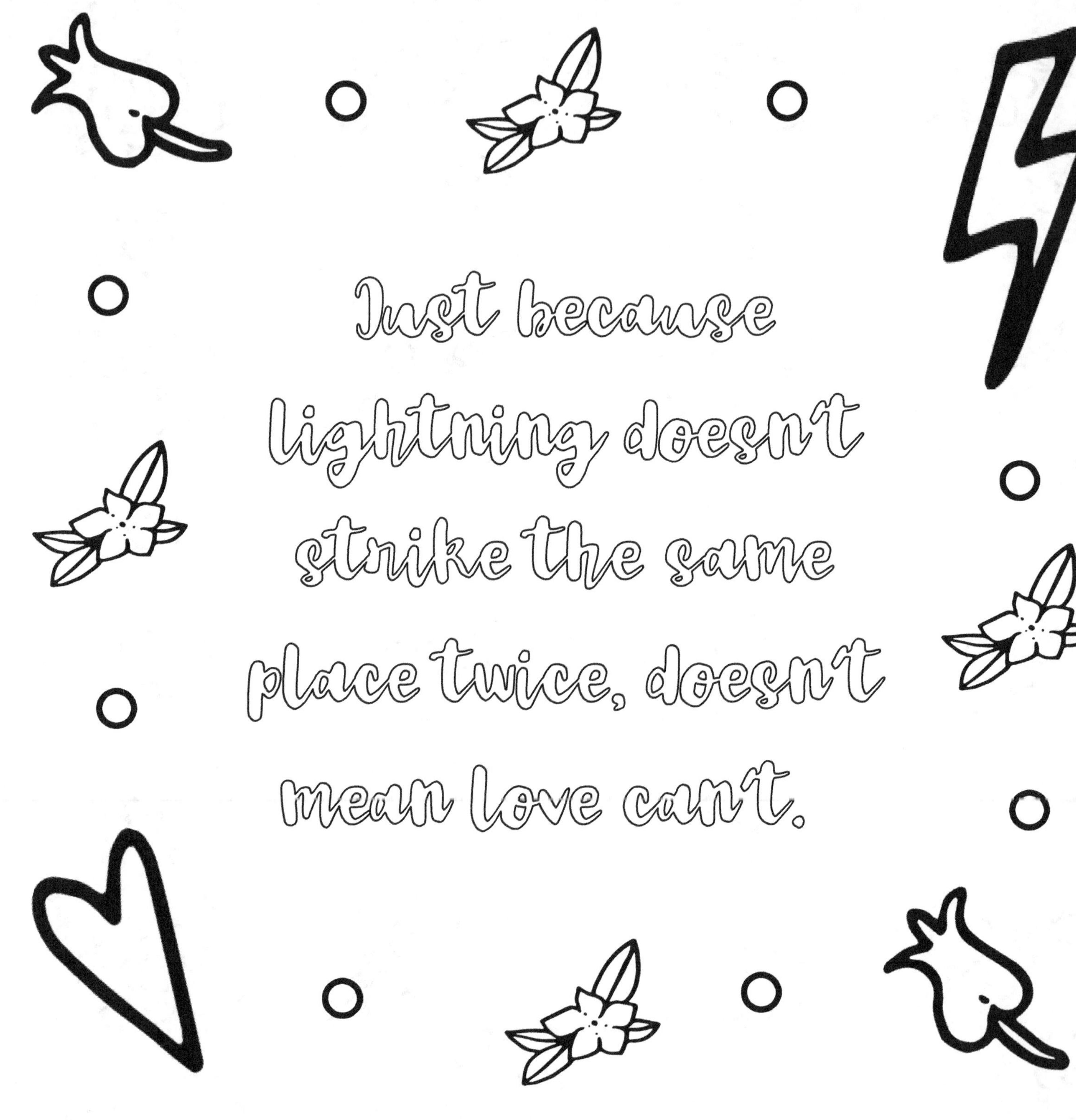

Just because lightning doesn't strike the same place twice, doesn't mean love can't.

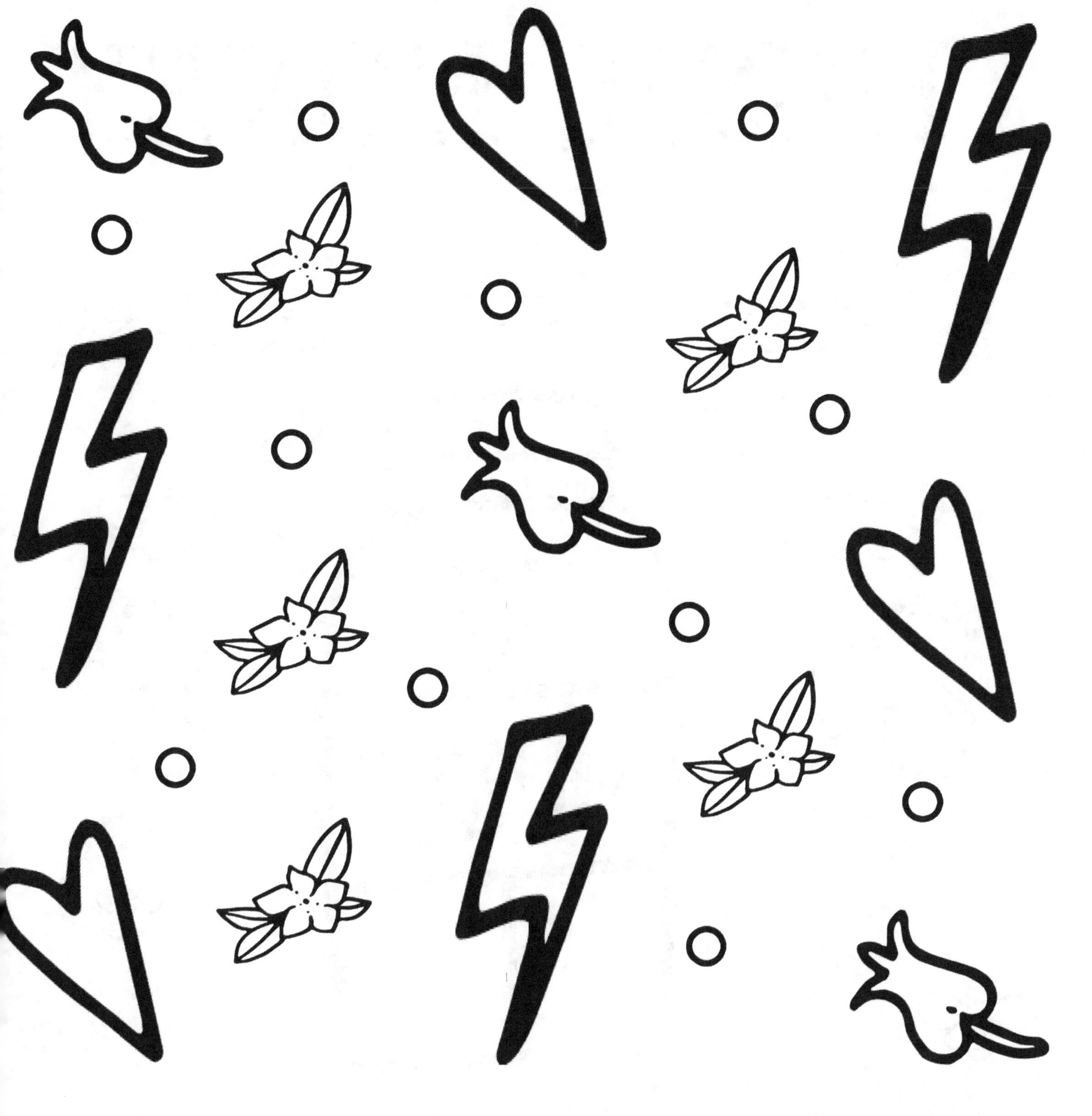

HUSH, HONEY

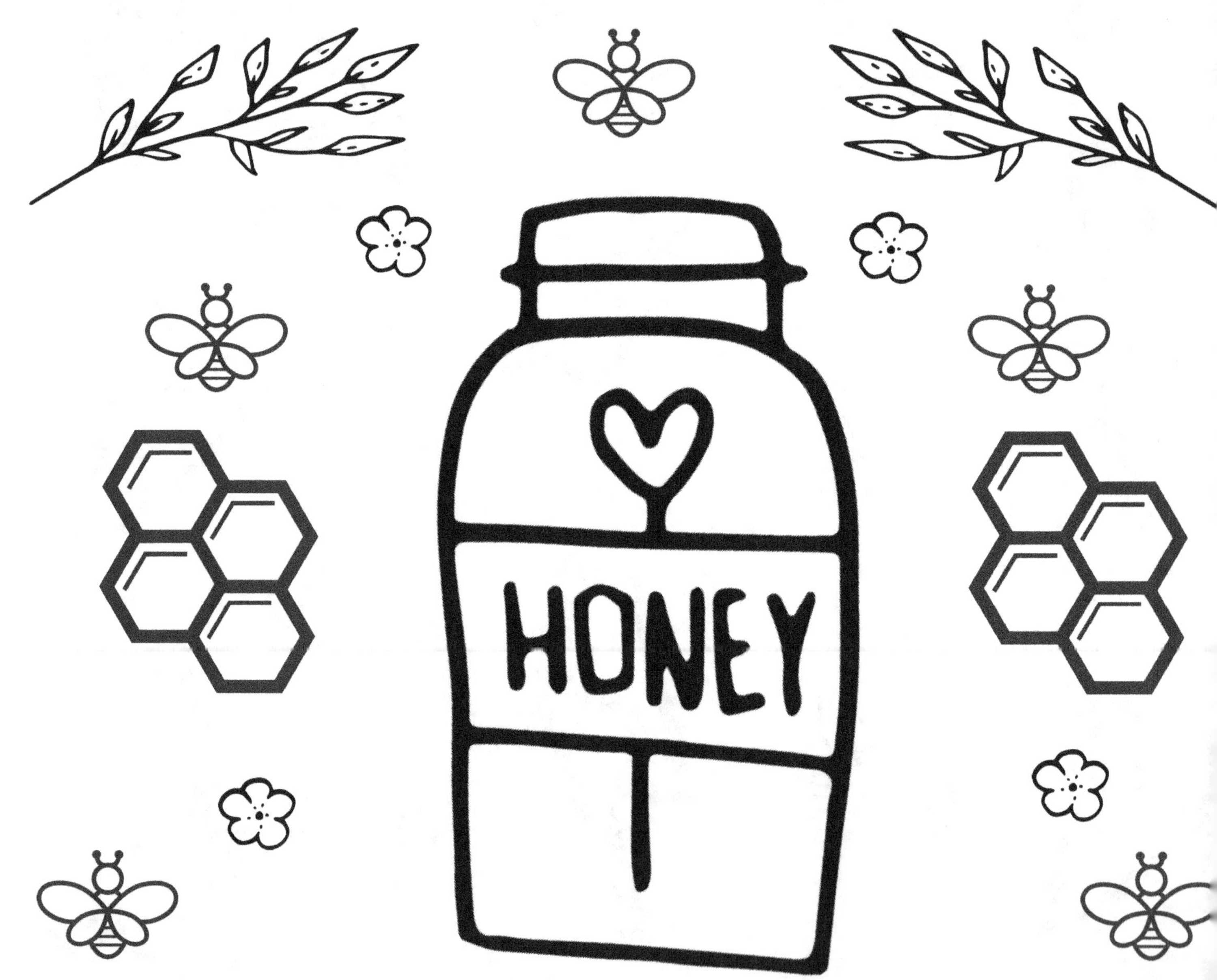

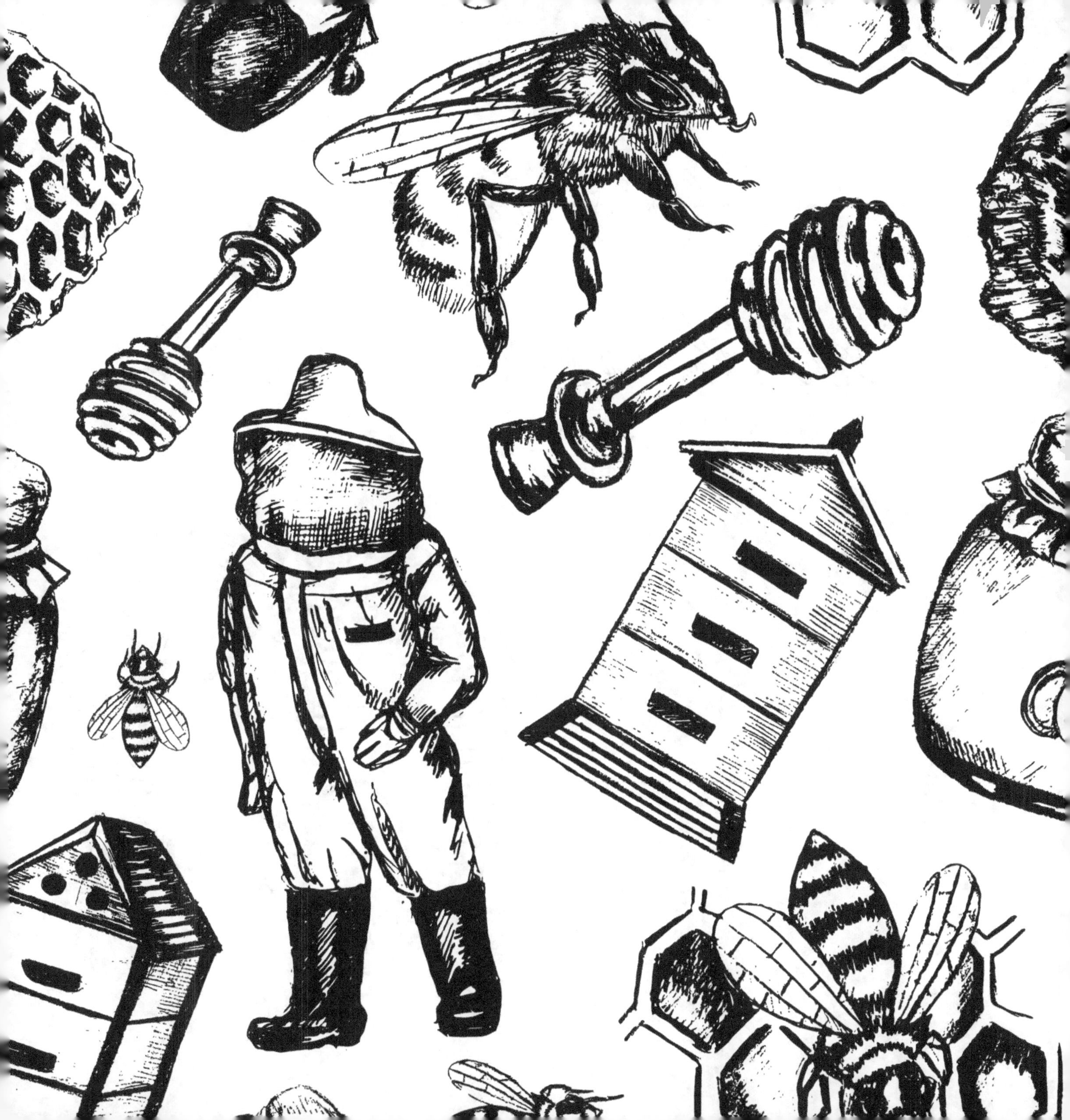

He's just a
peach gone to rot.

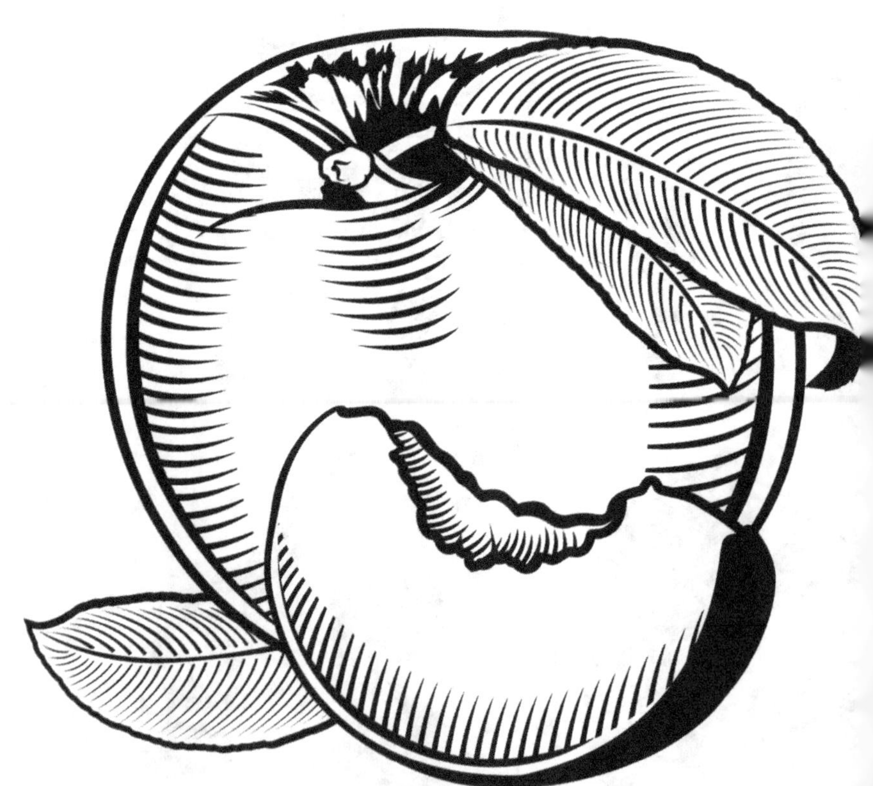

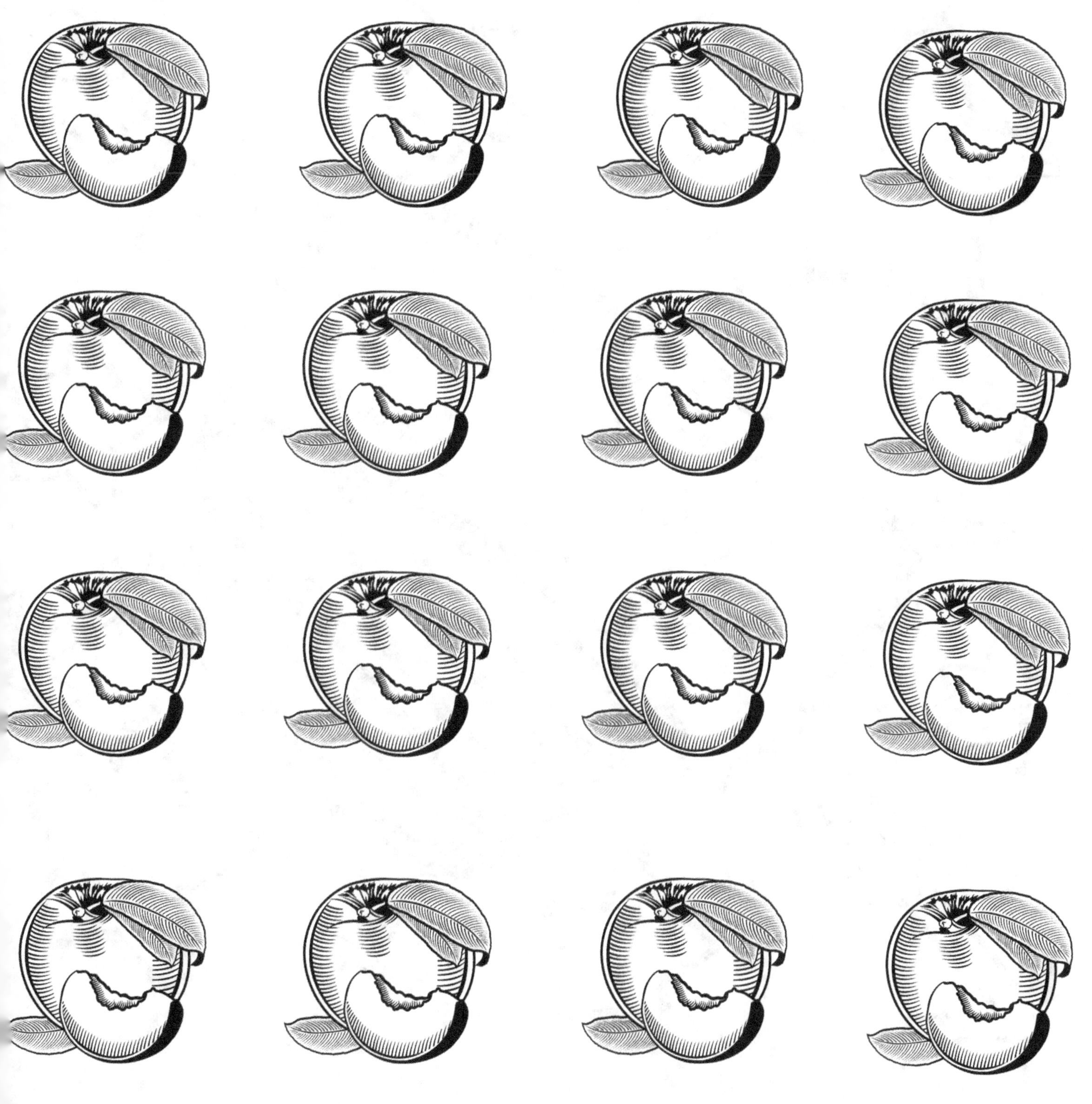

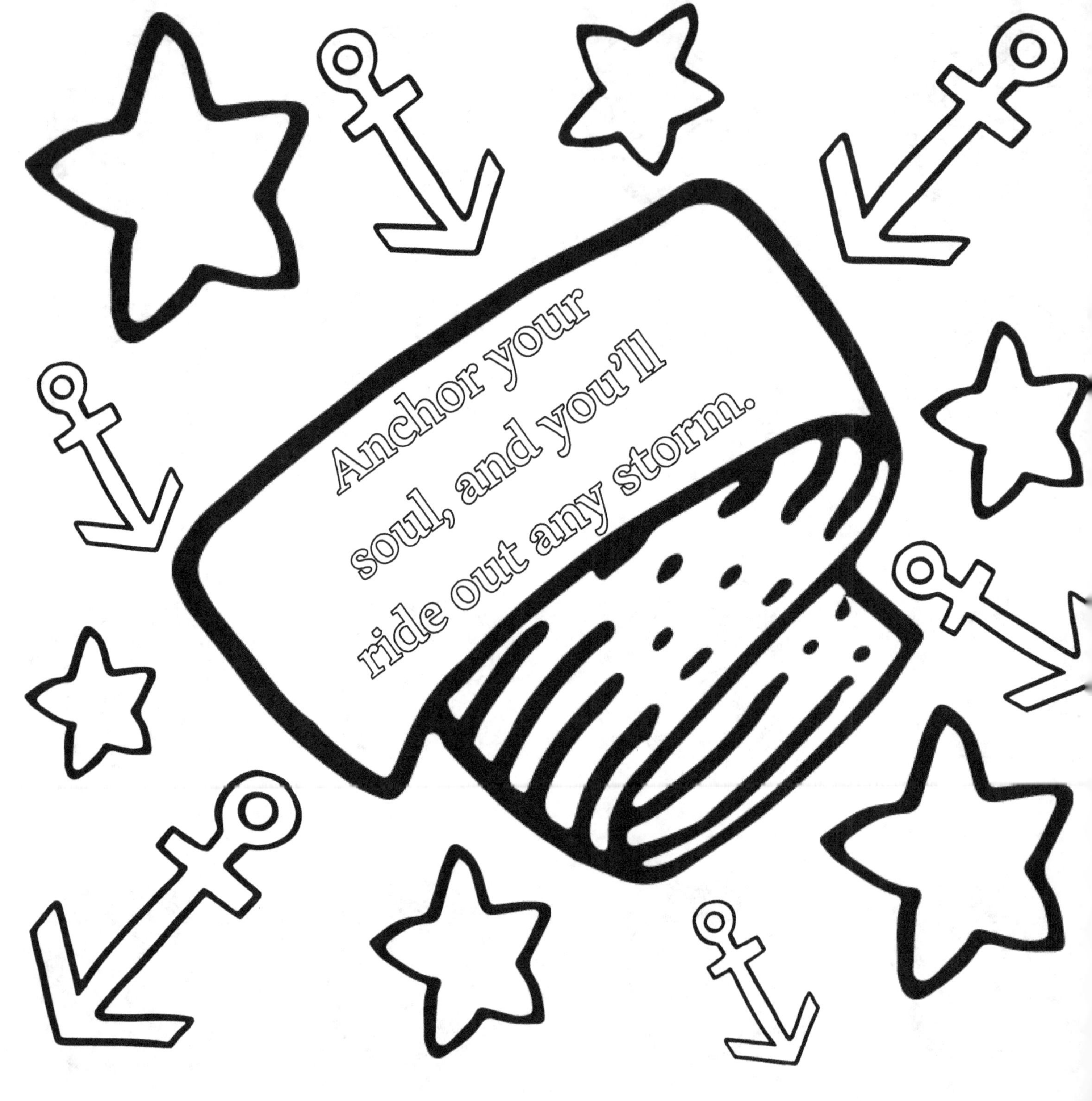

Anchor your soul, and you'll ride out any storm.

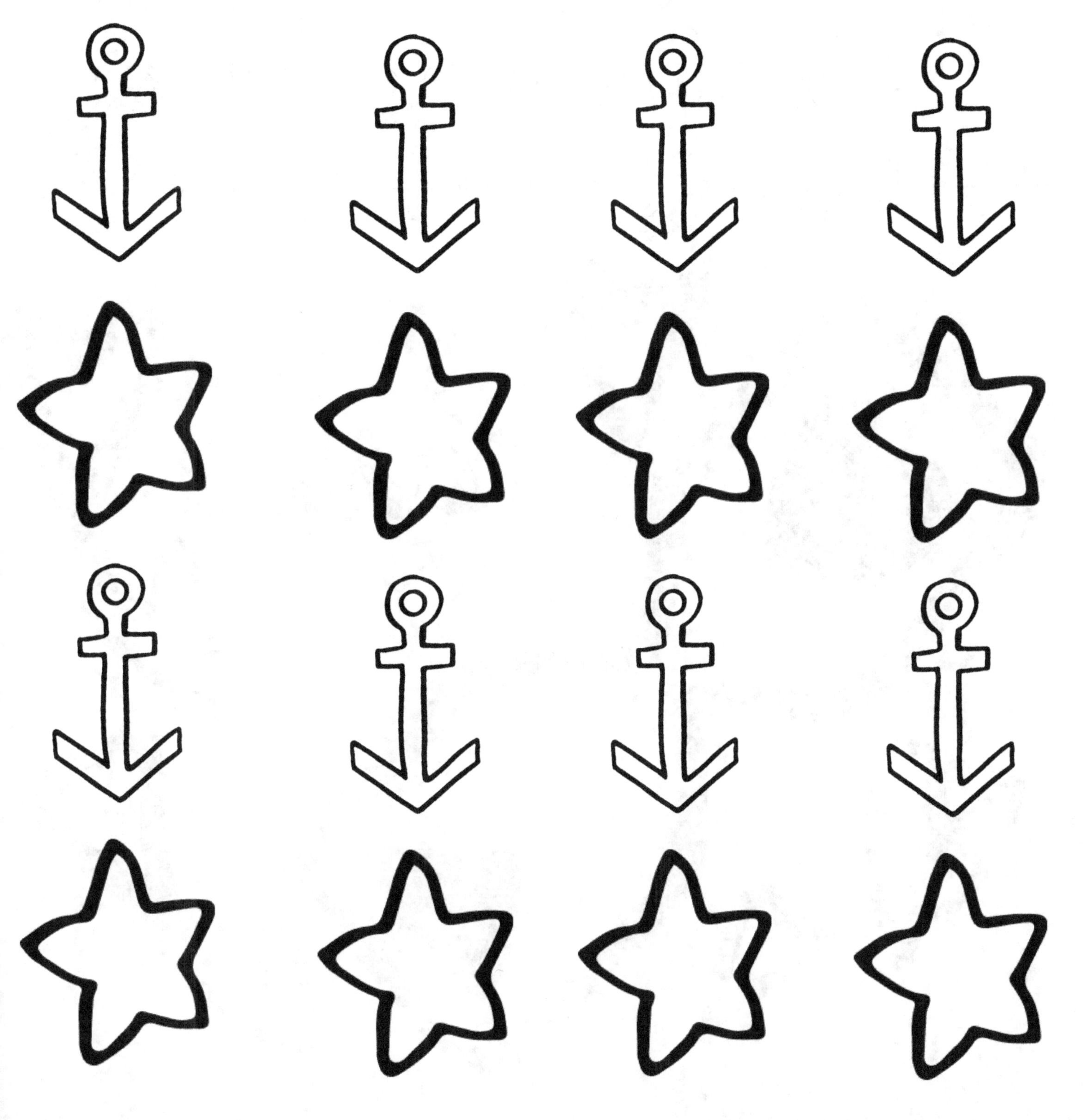

Absence makes the heart grow fonder.

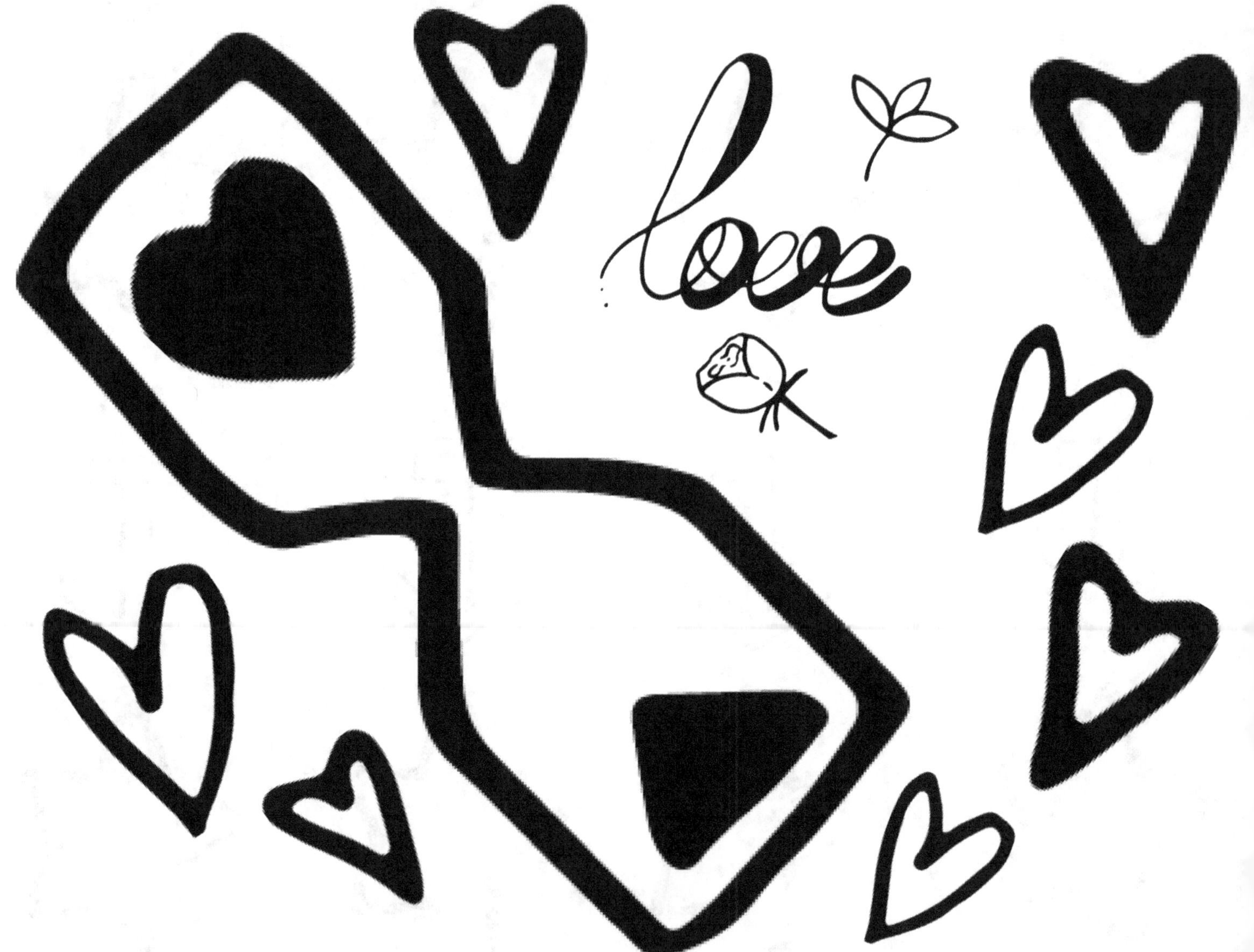

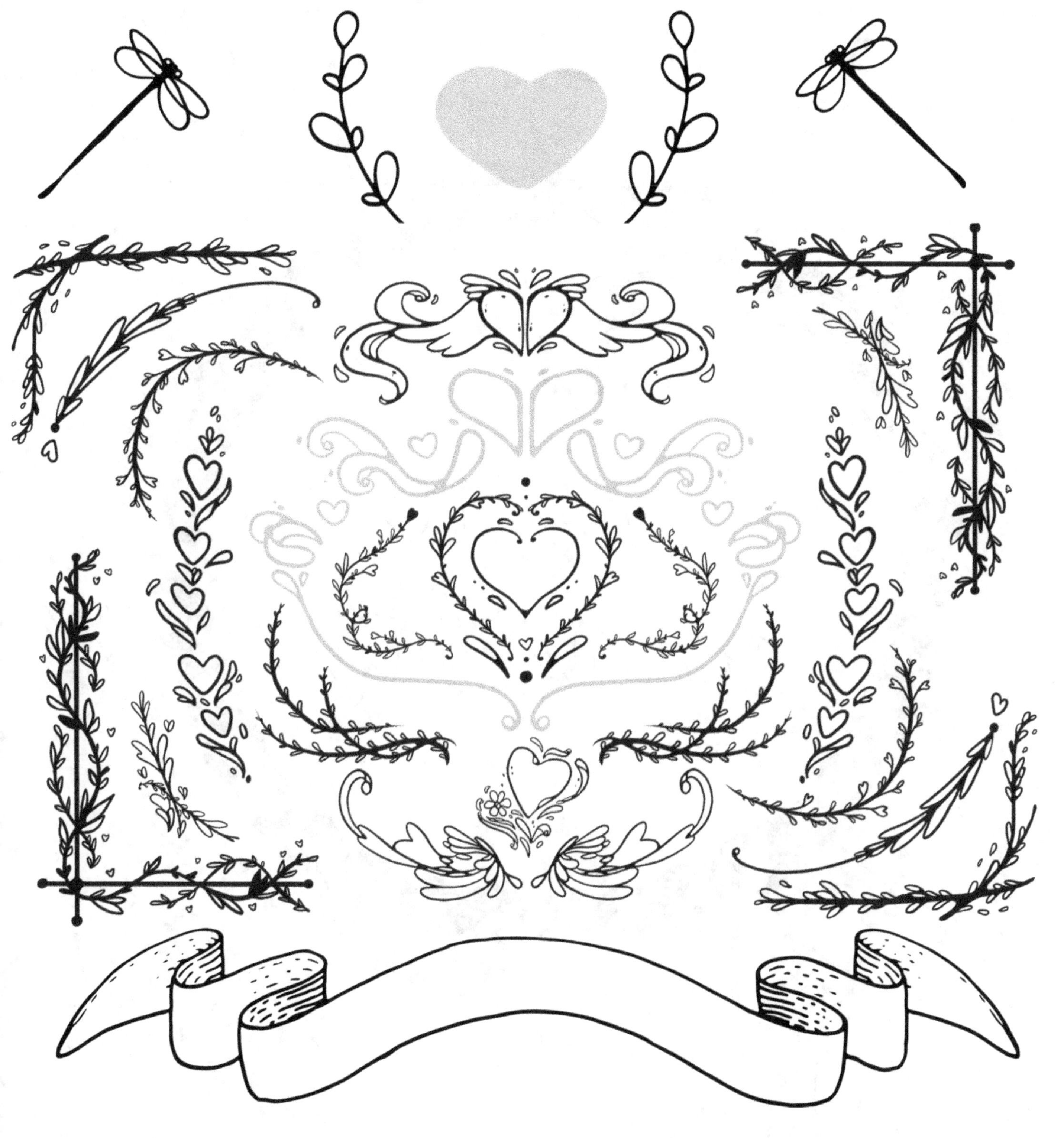

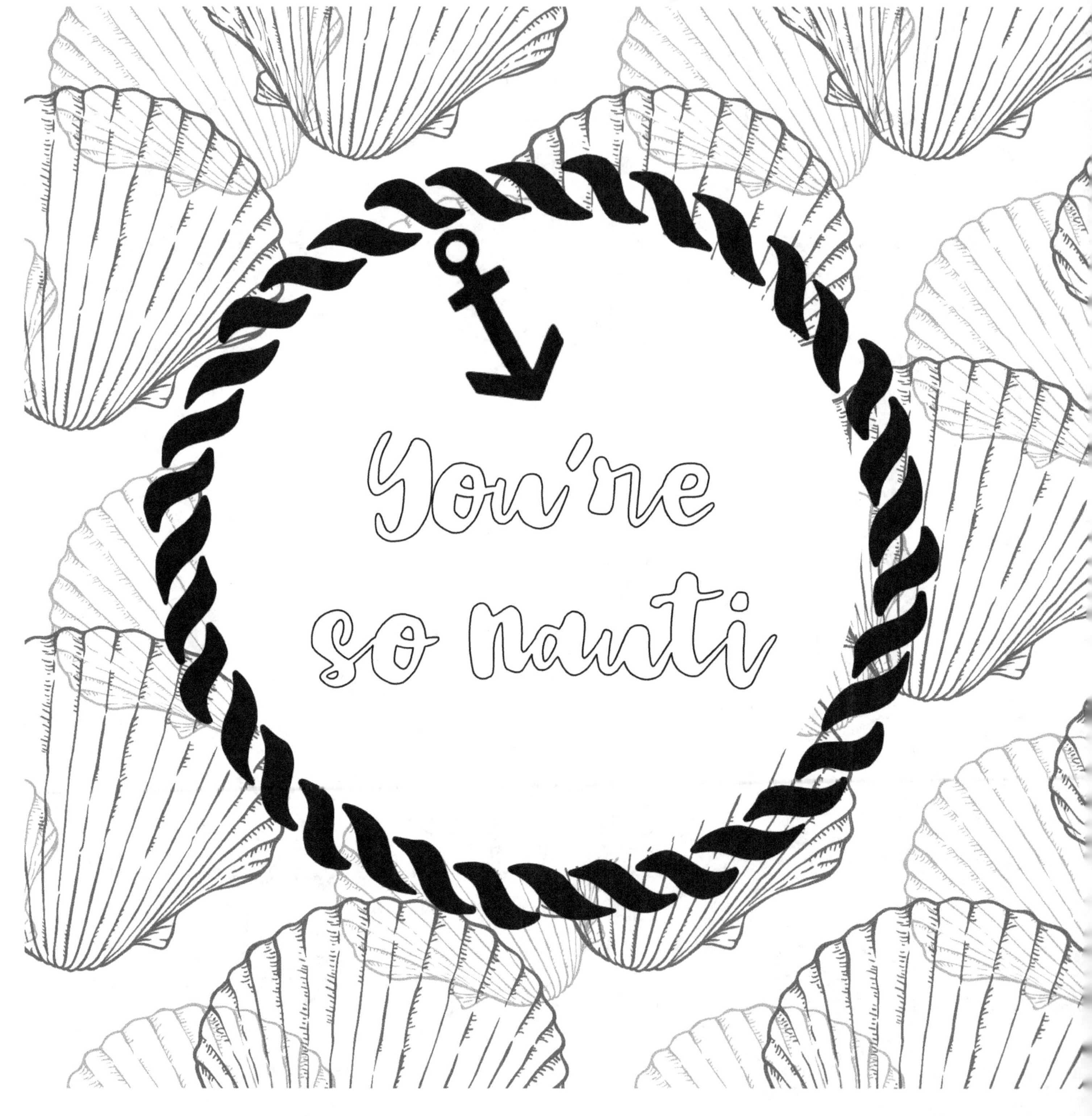
You're
so nauti

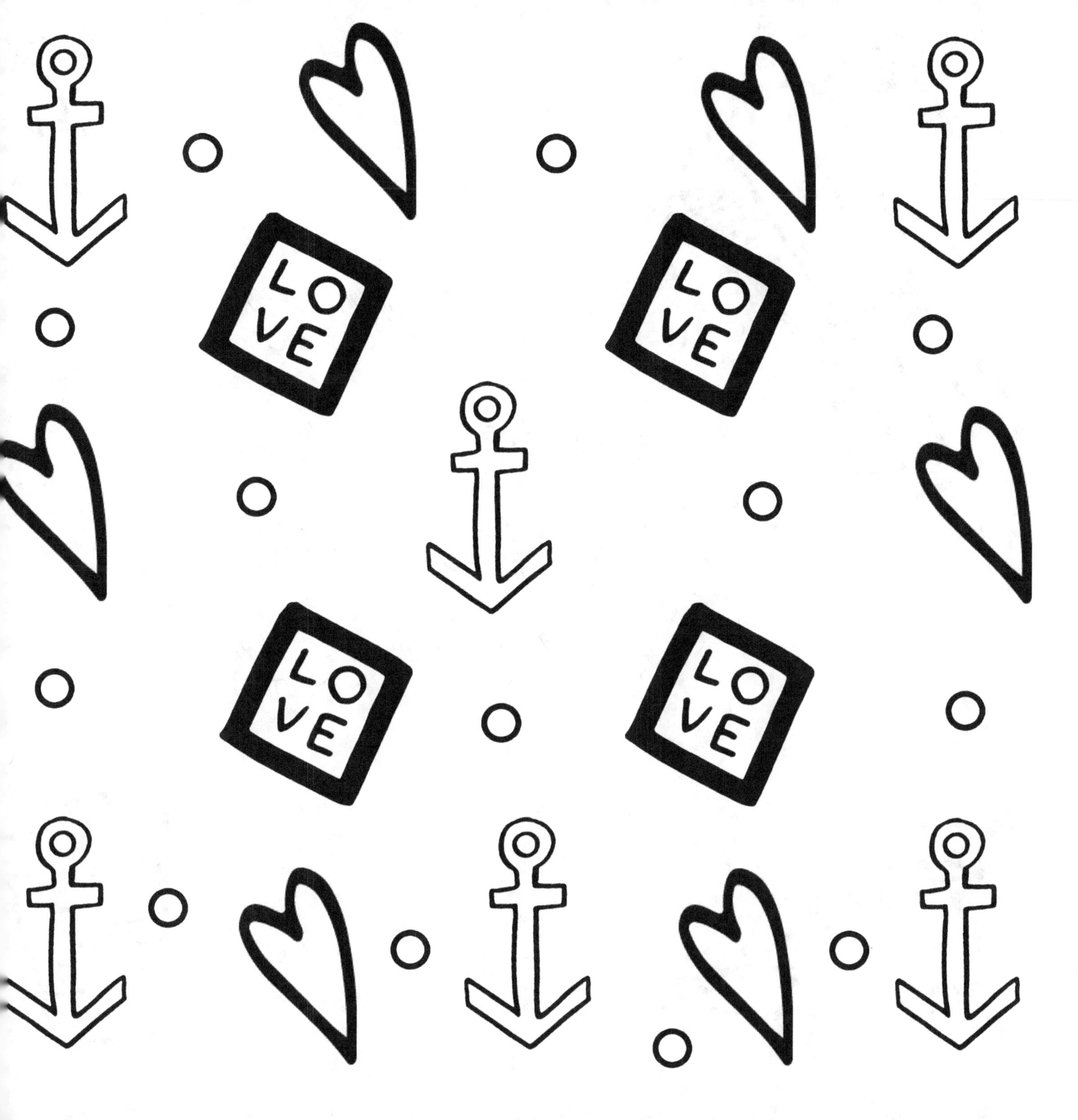

LO VE
LO VE
LO VE
LO VE

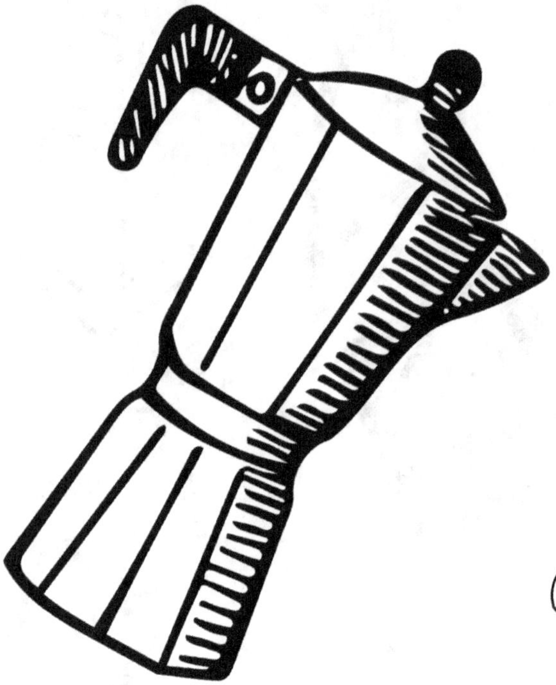

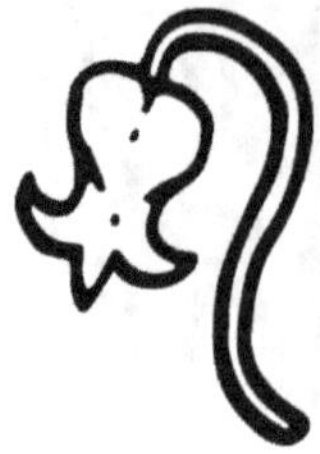

Spill it, hon—what's on your mind, not the coffee.

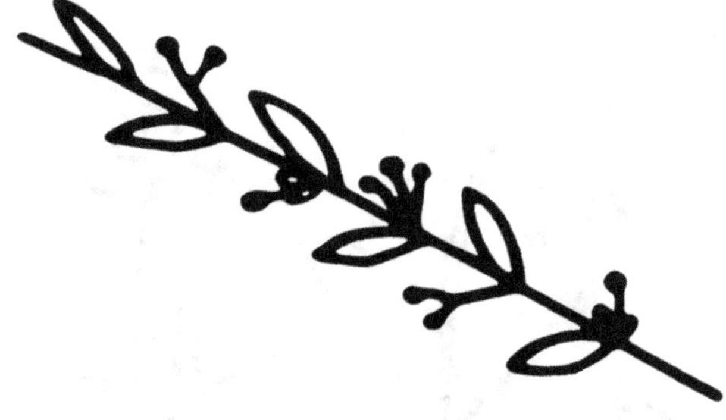

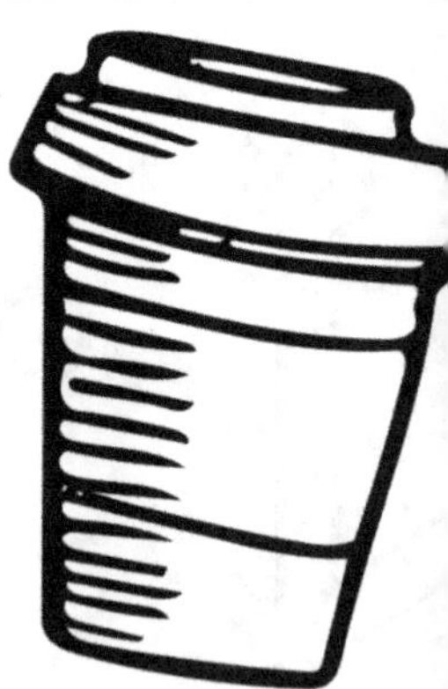

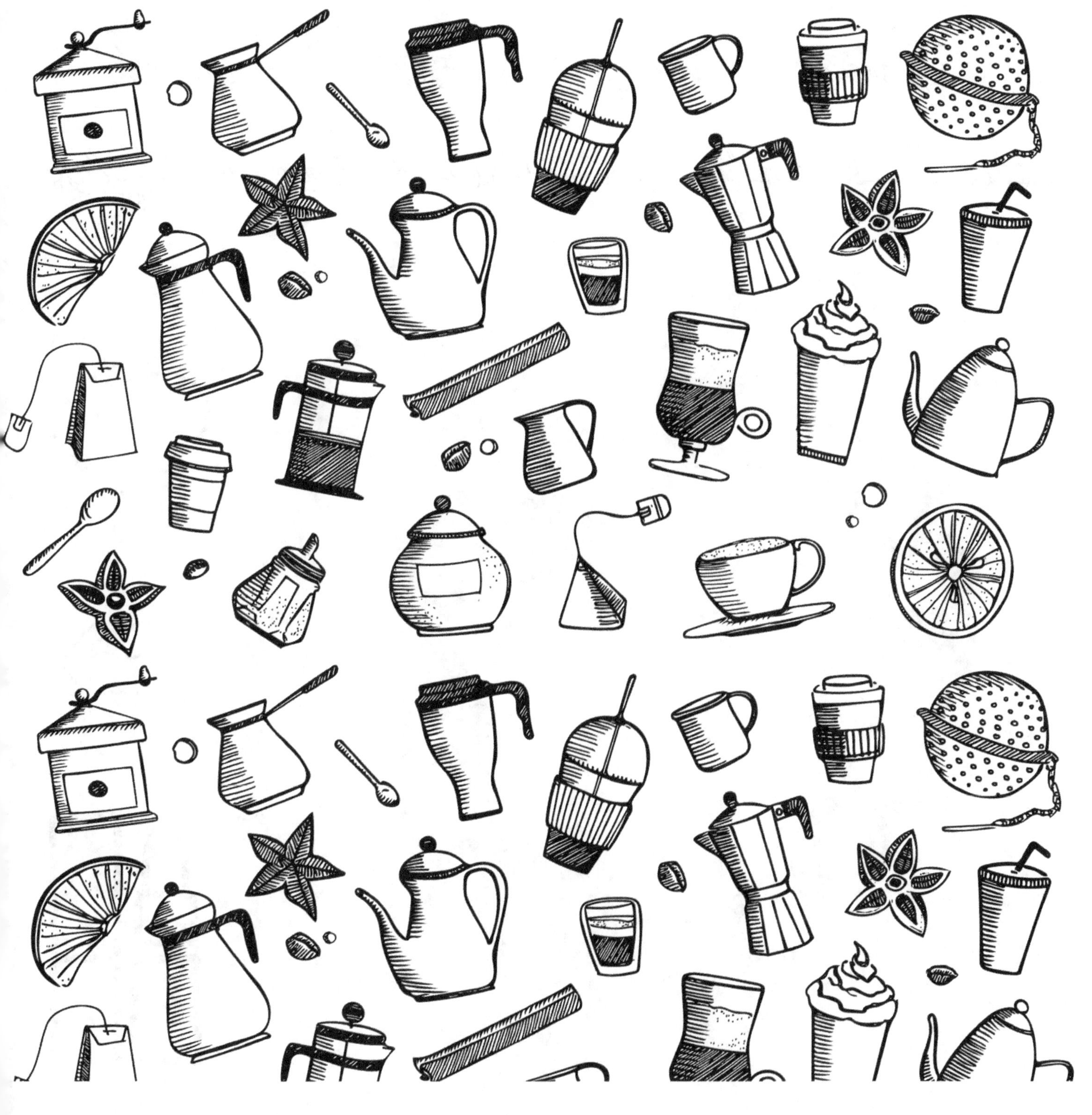

Good manners, red lipstick and pearls go with every outfit.

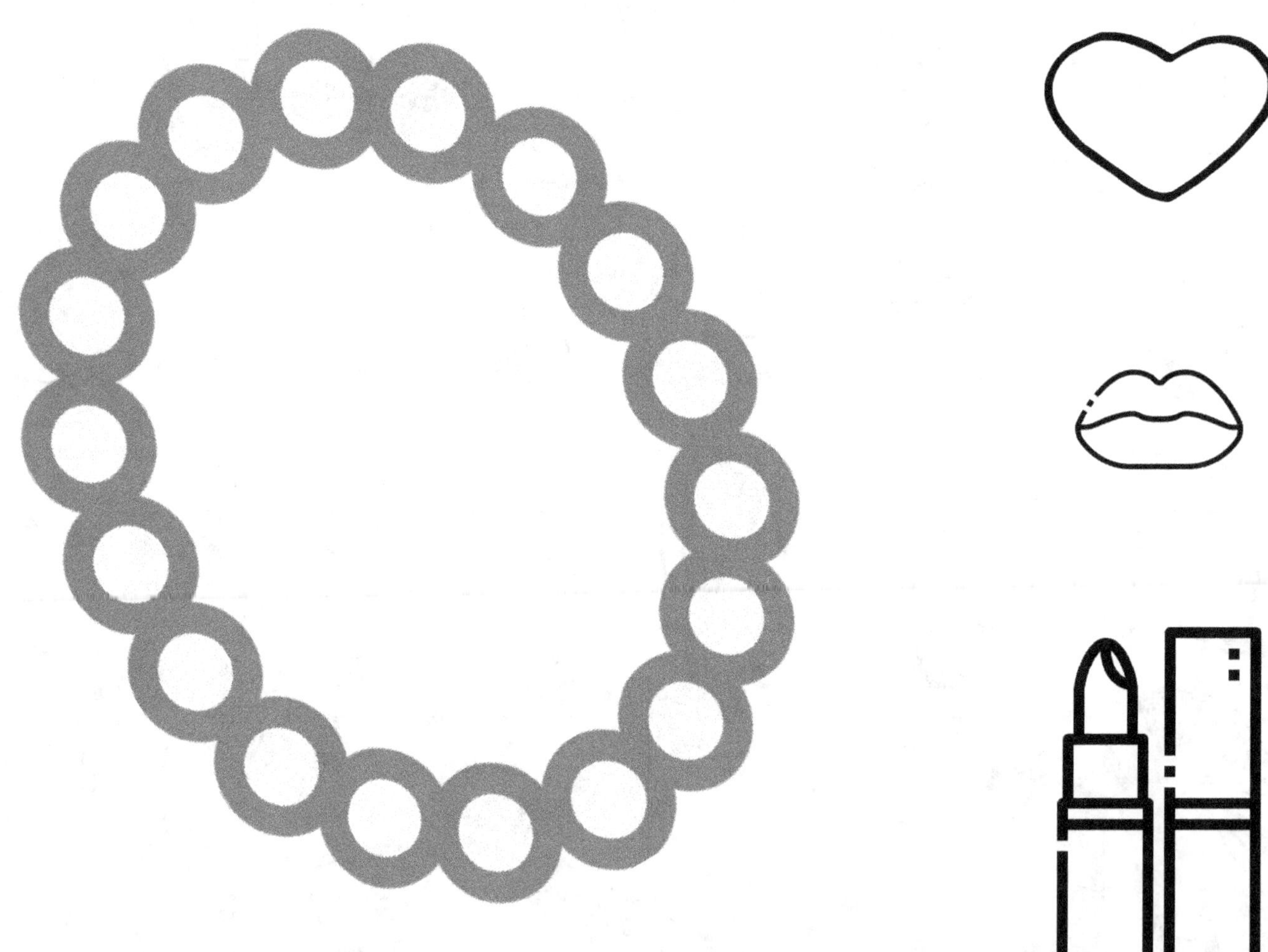

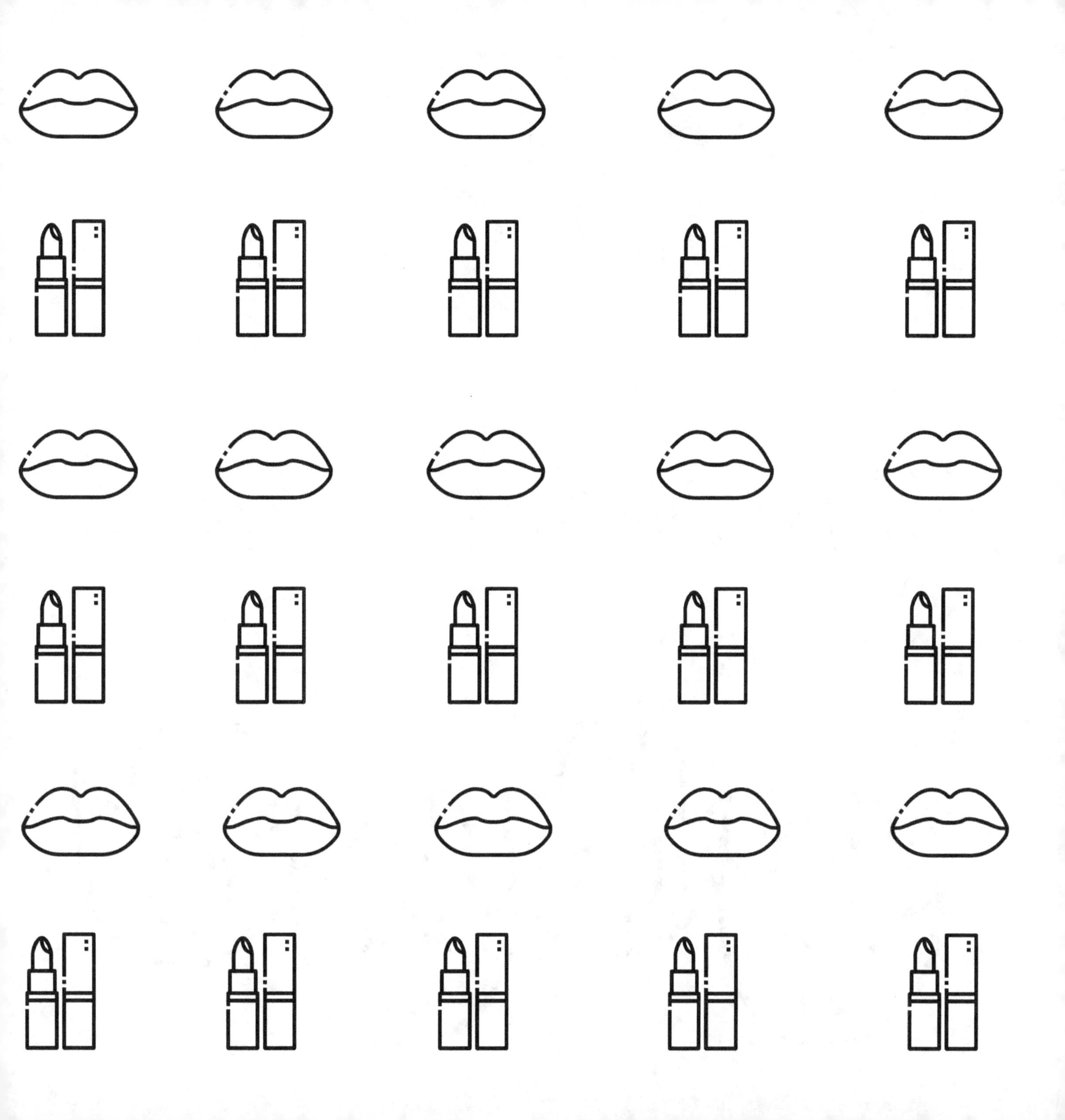

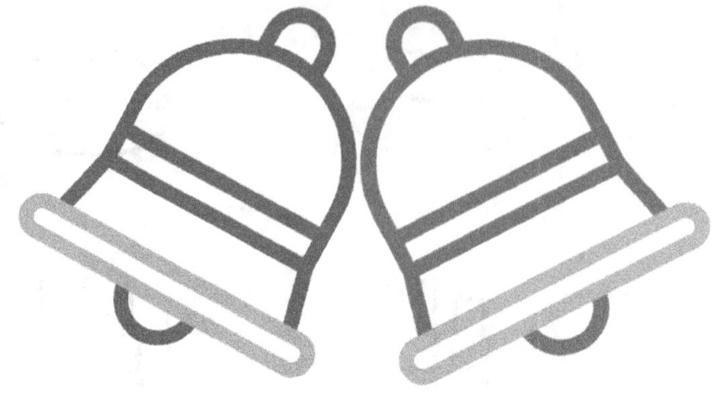

Well, Hell's bells.

Life should be

like tea...sweet

with just a hint

of bitterness.

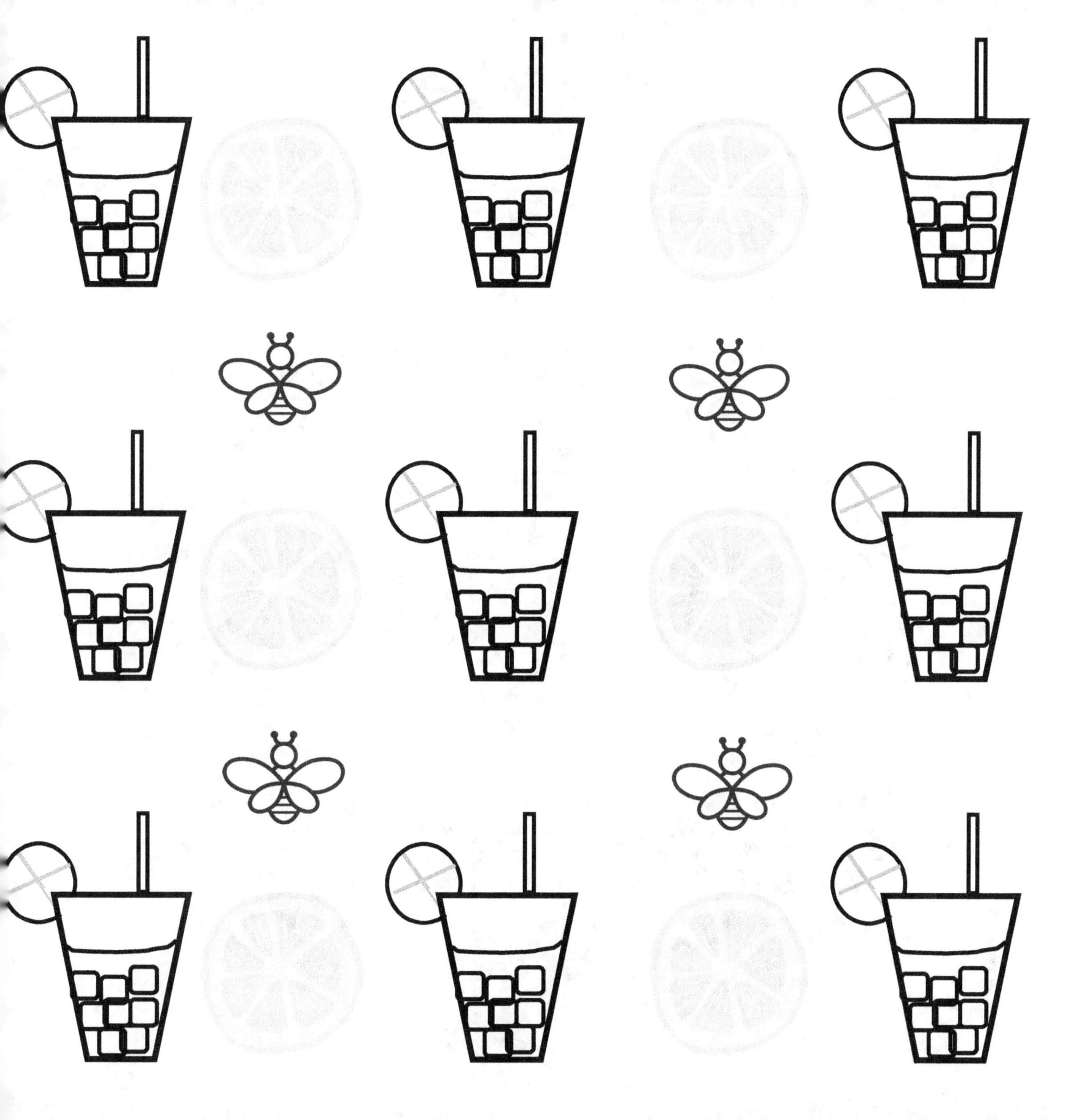

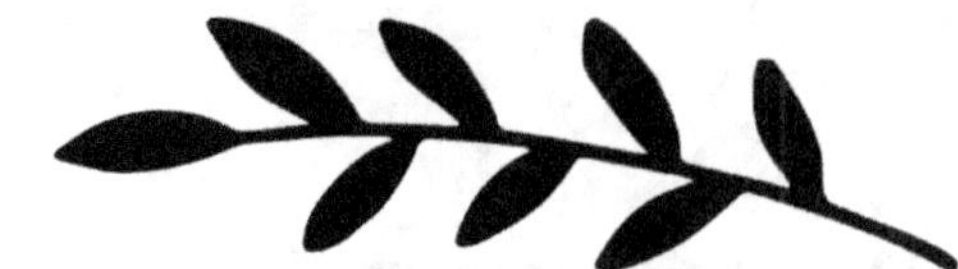

As sweet as pie

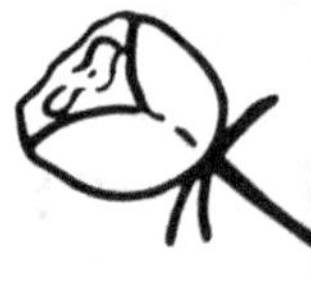

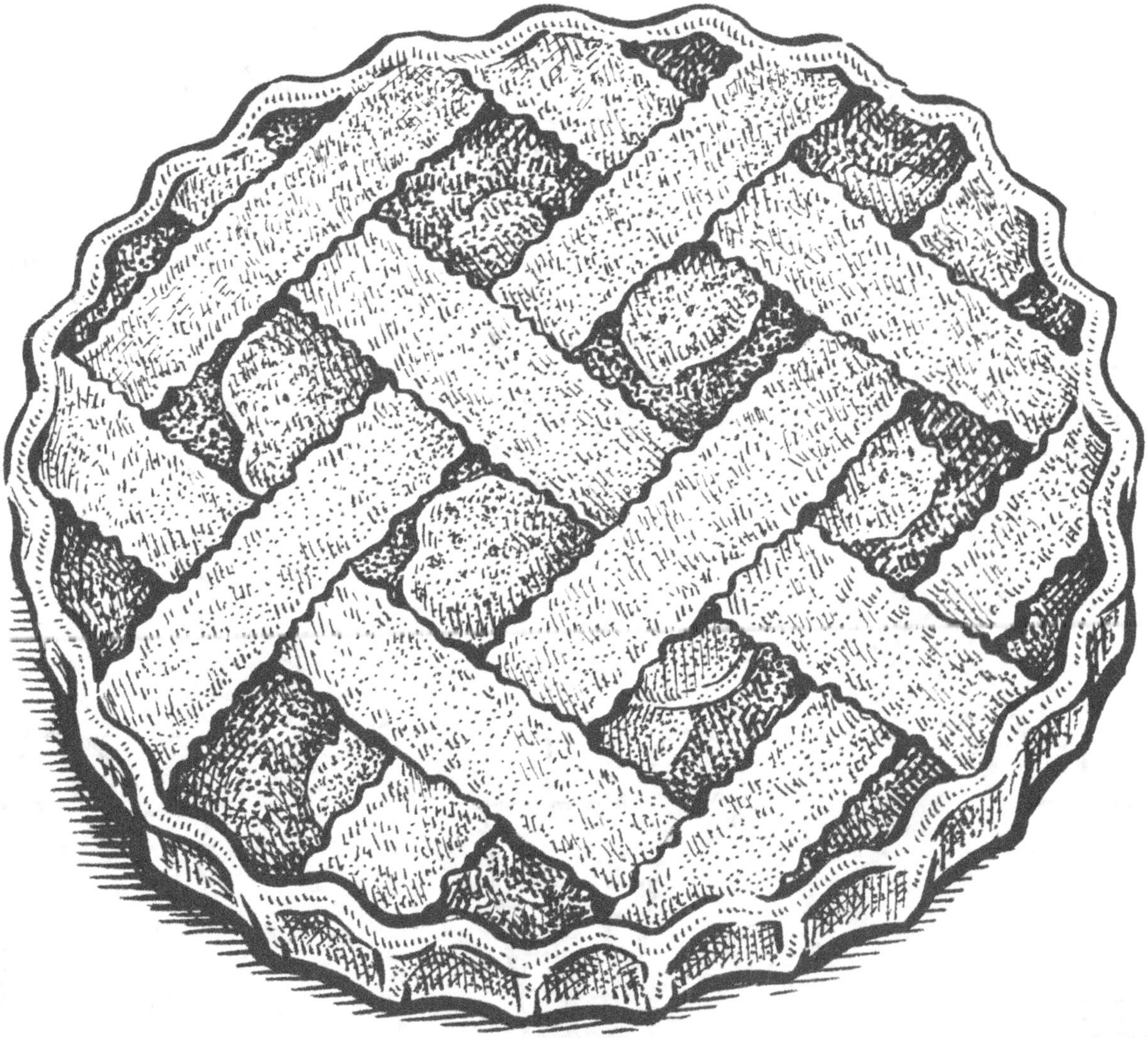

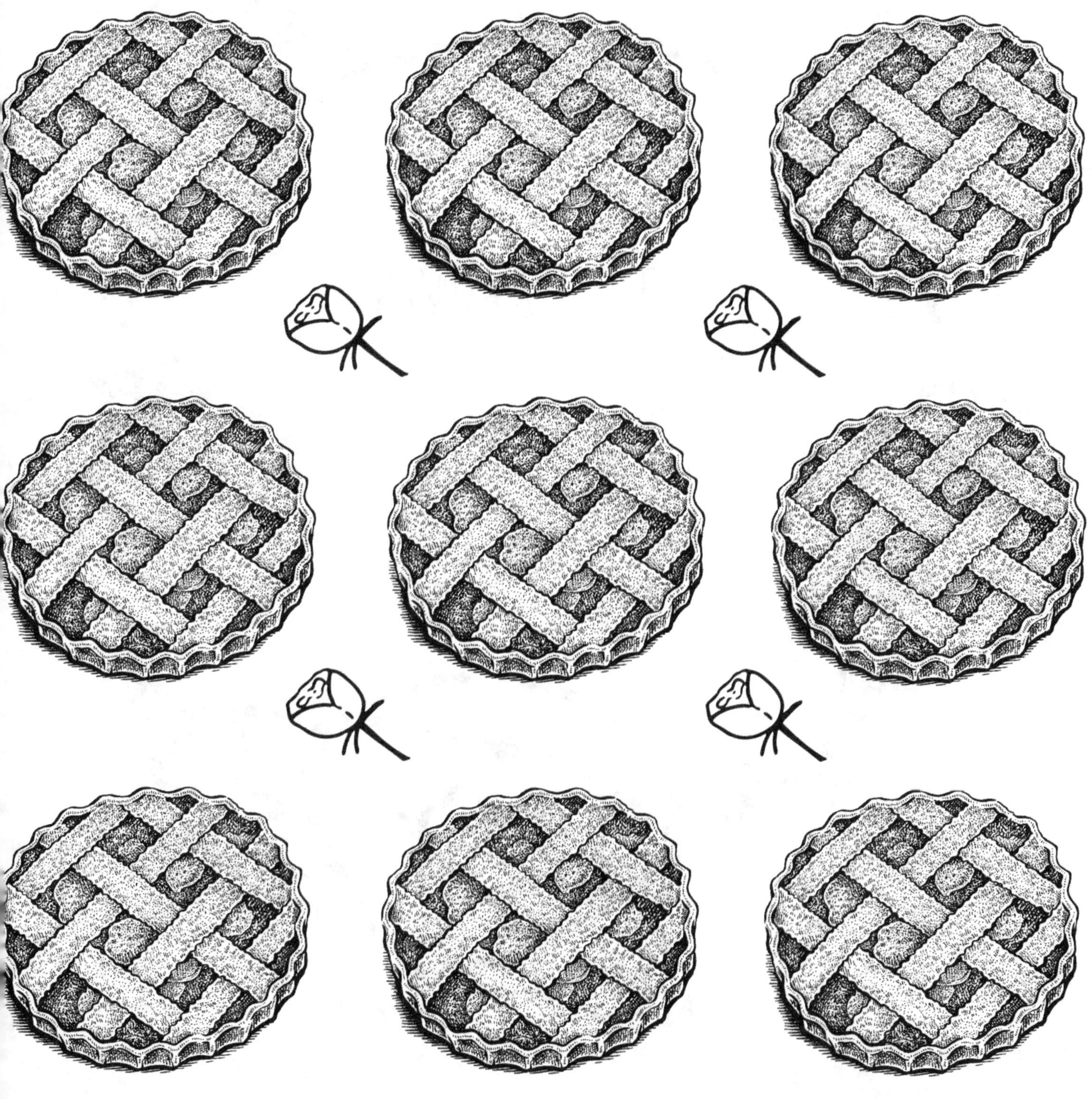

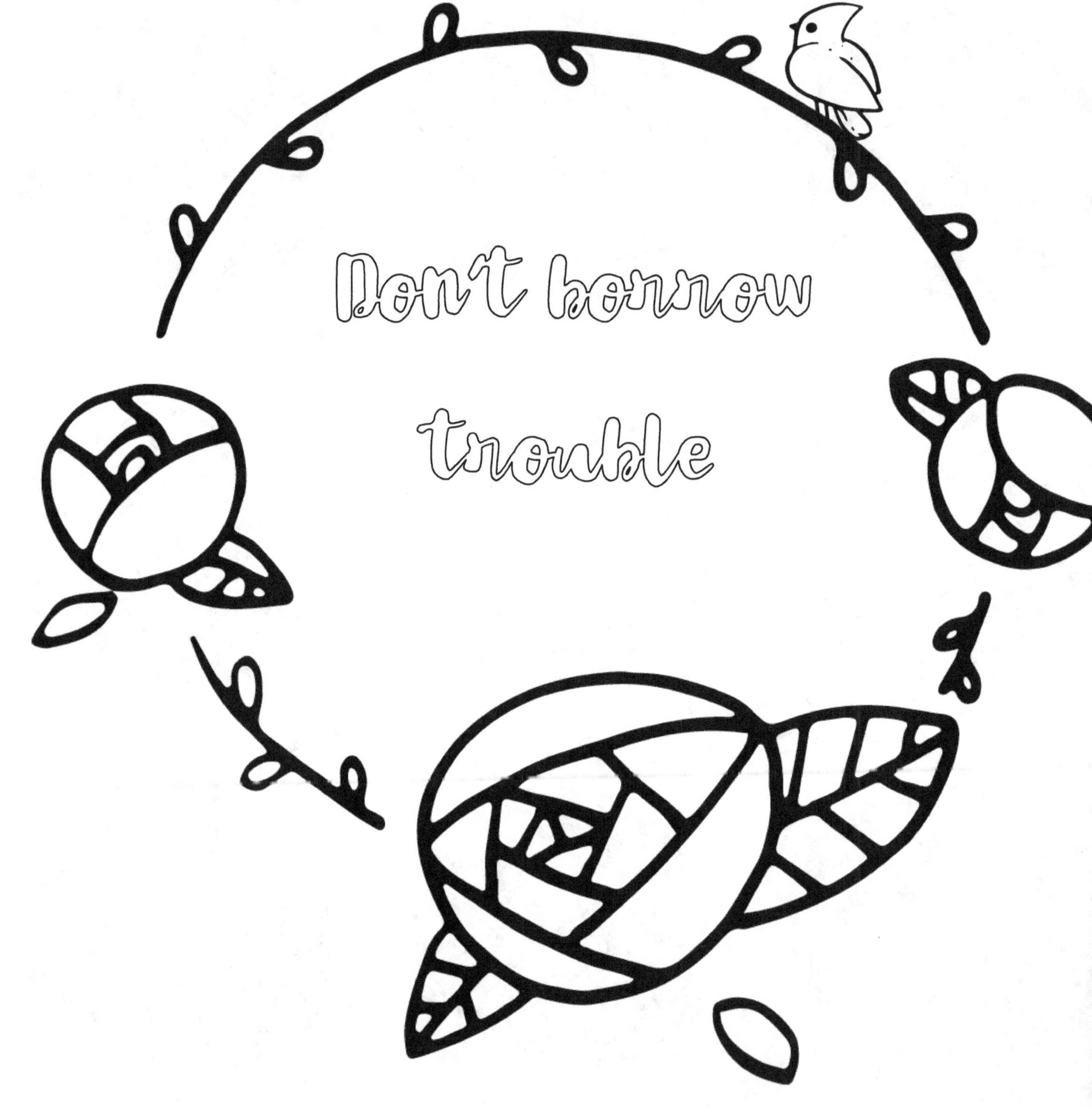
Don't borrow
trouble

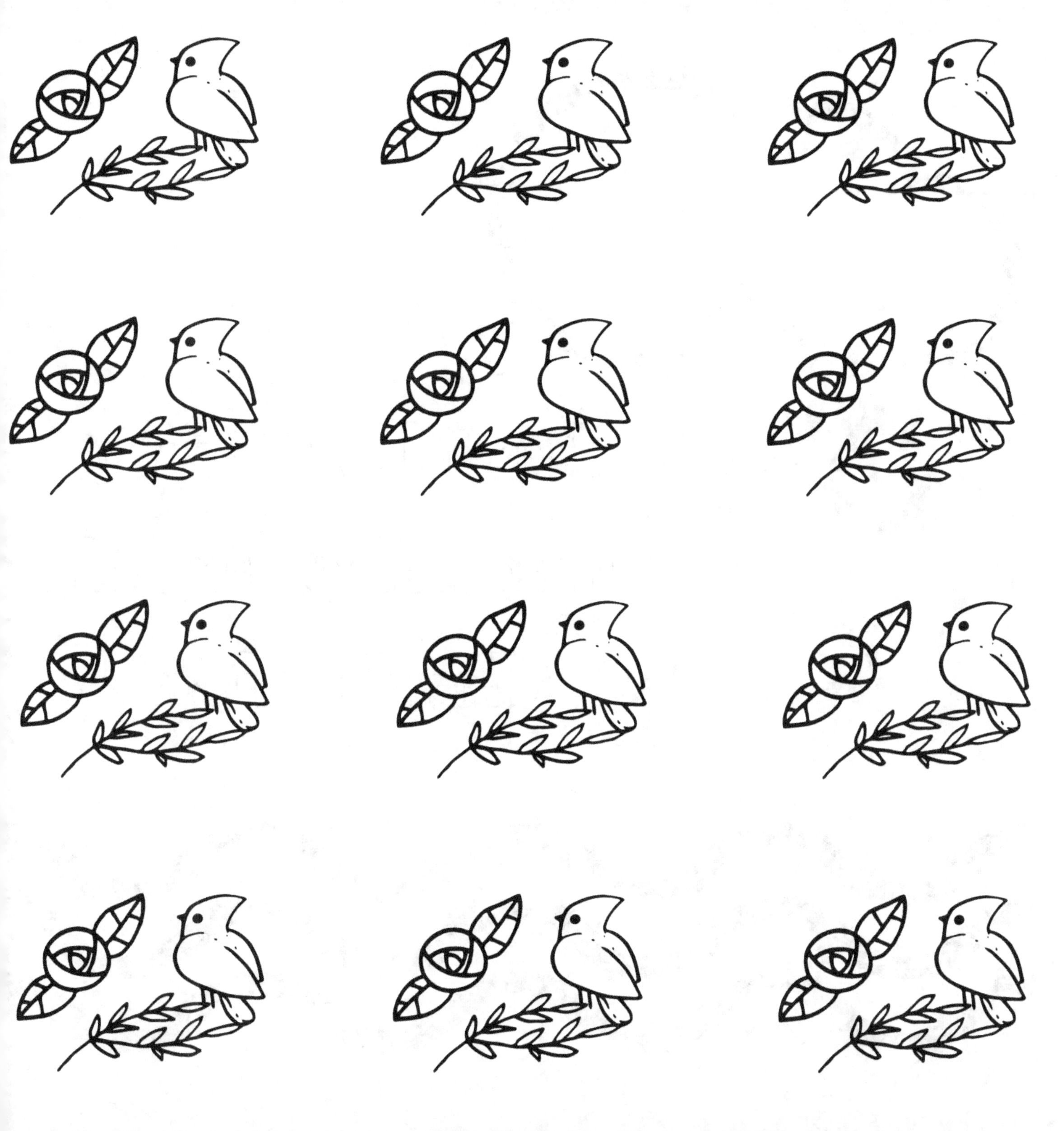

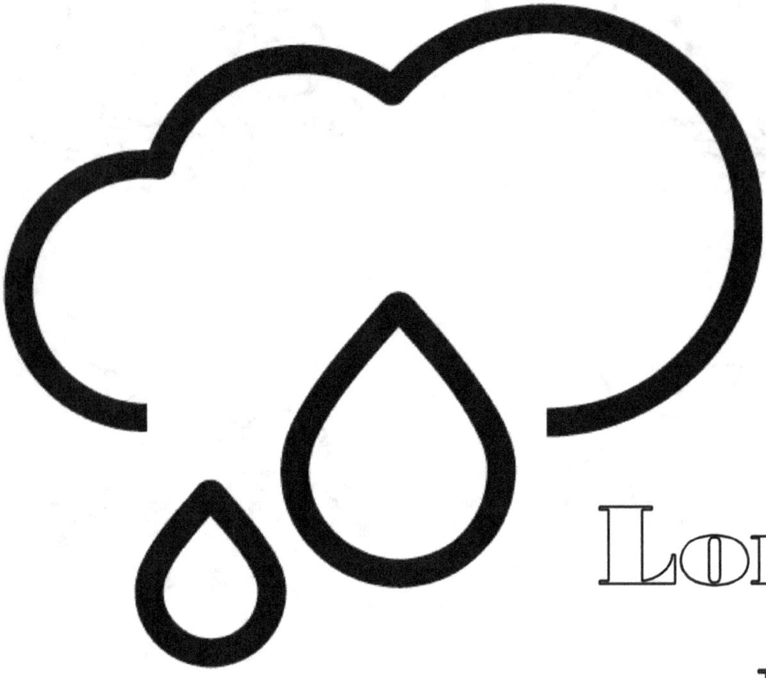

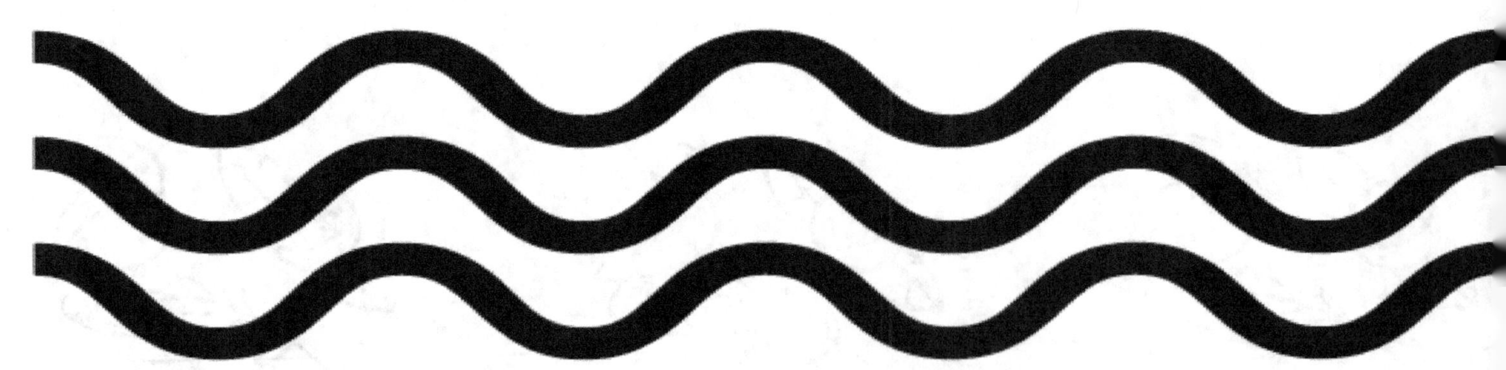

Lord willing,
and the creek
don't rise.

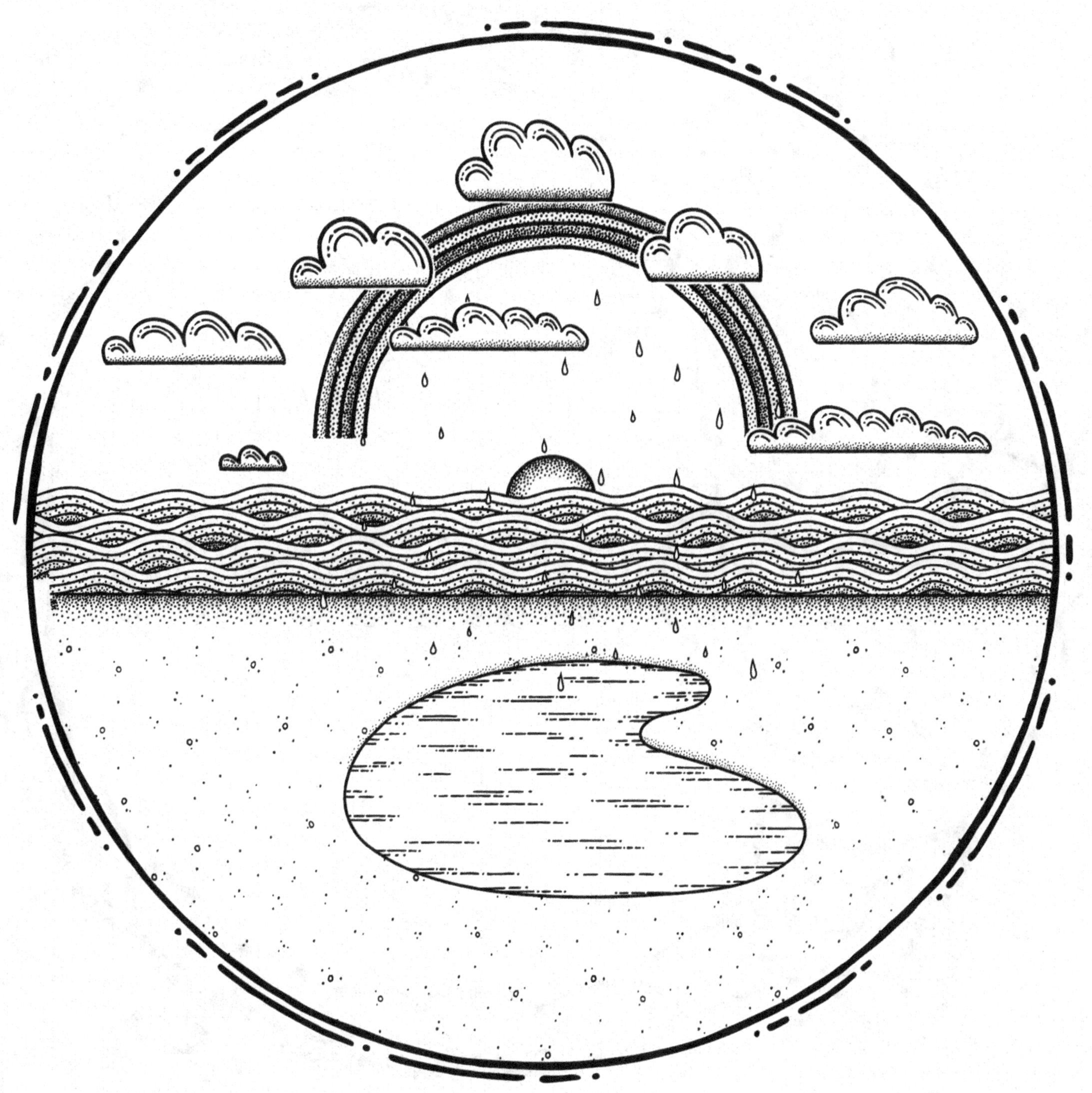

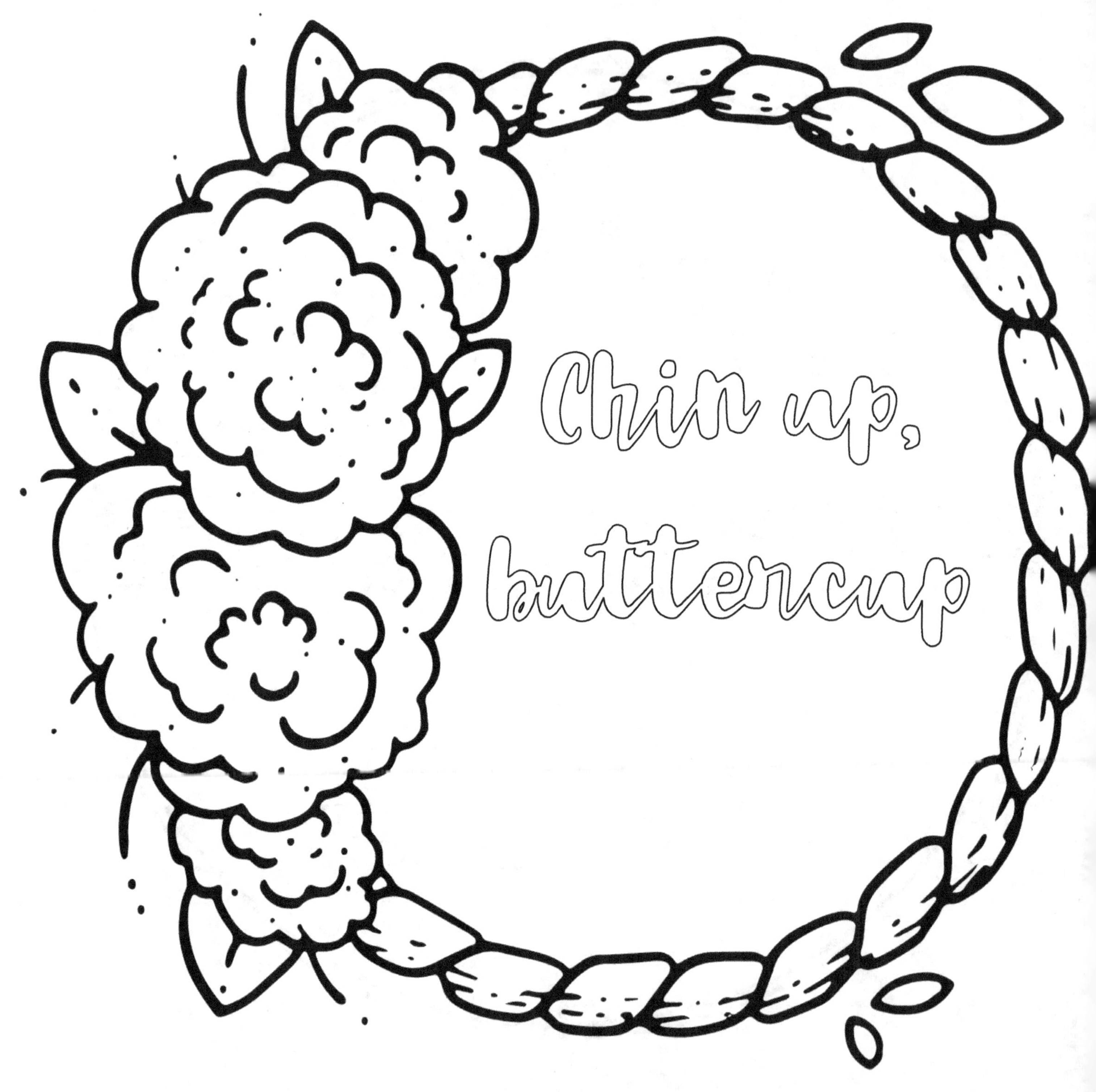

Chin up,
buttercup

You're barking up
the wrong tree.

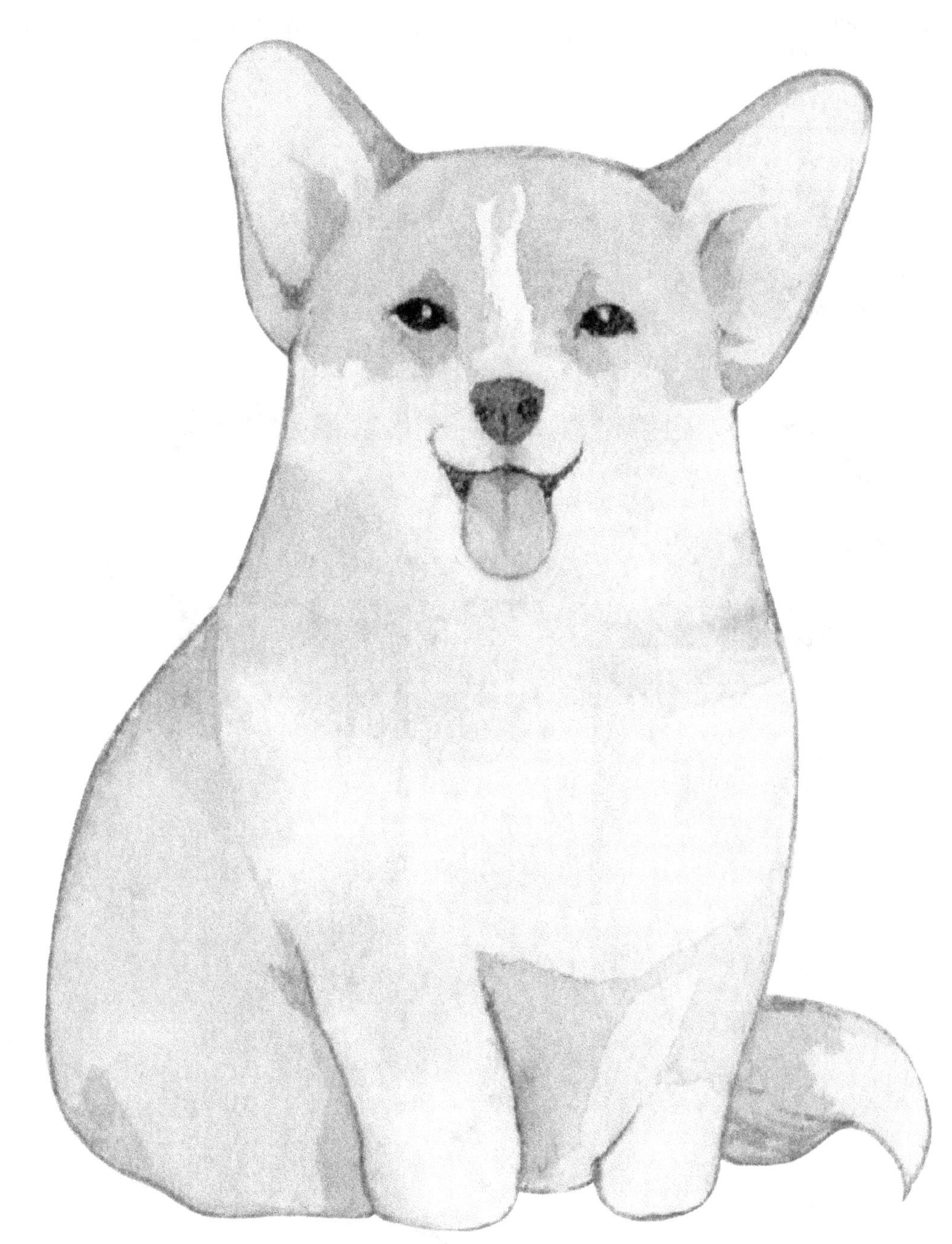

Lord, have mercy!

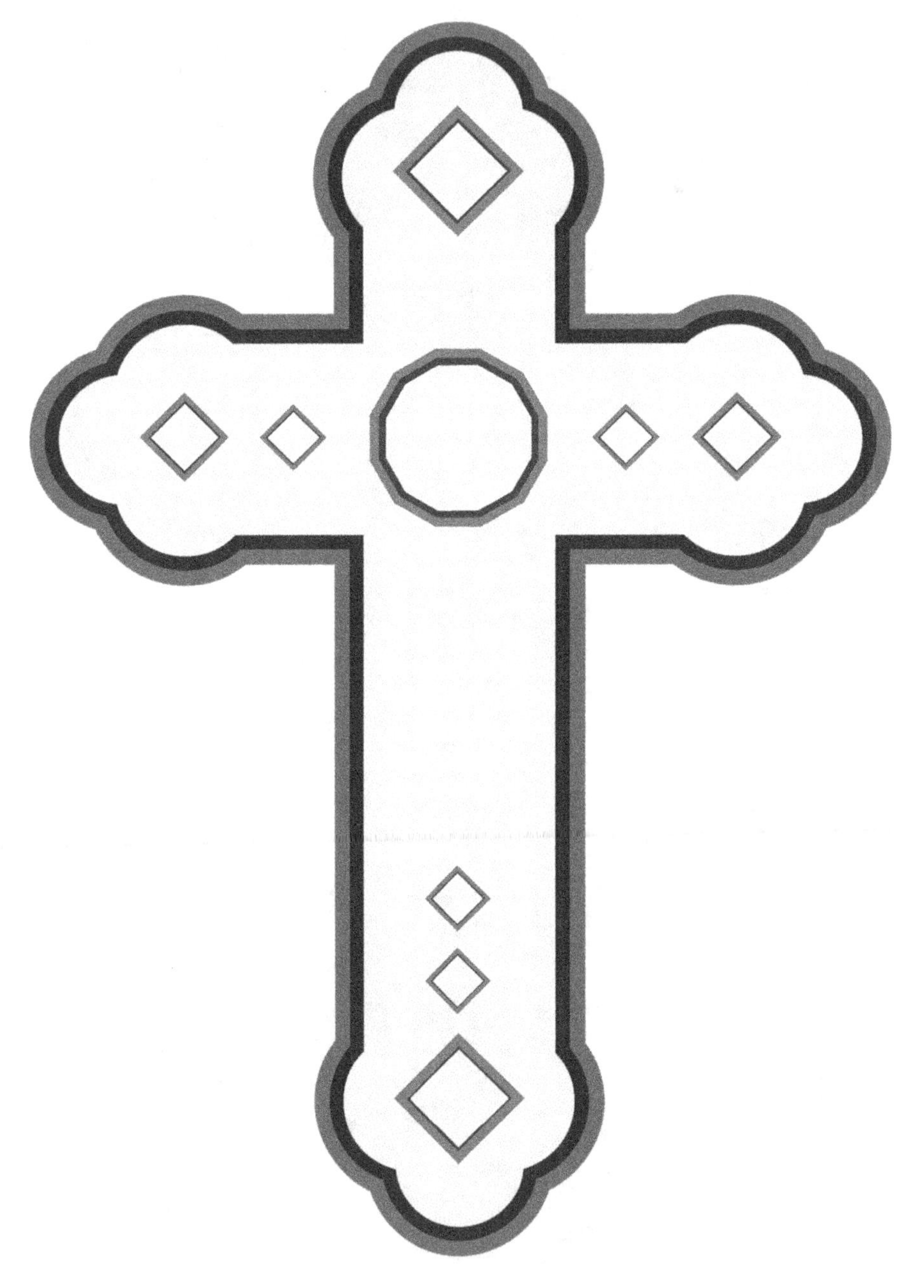

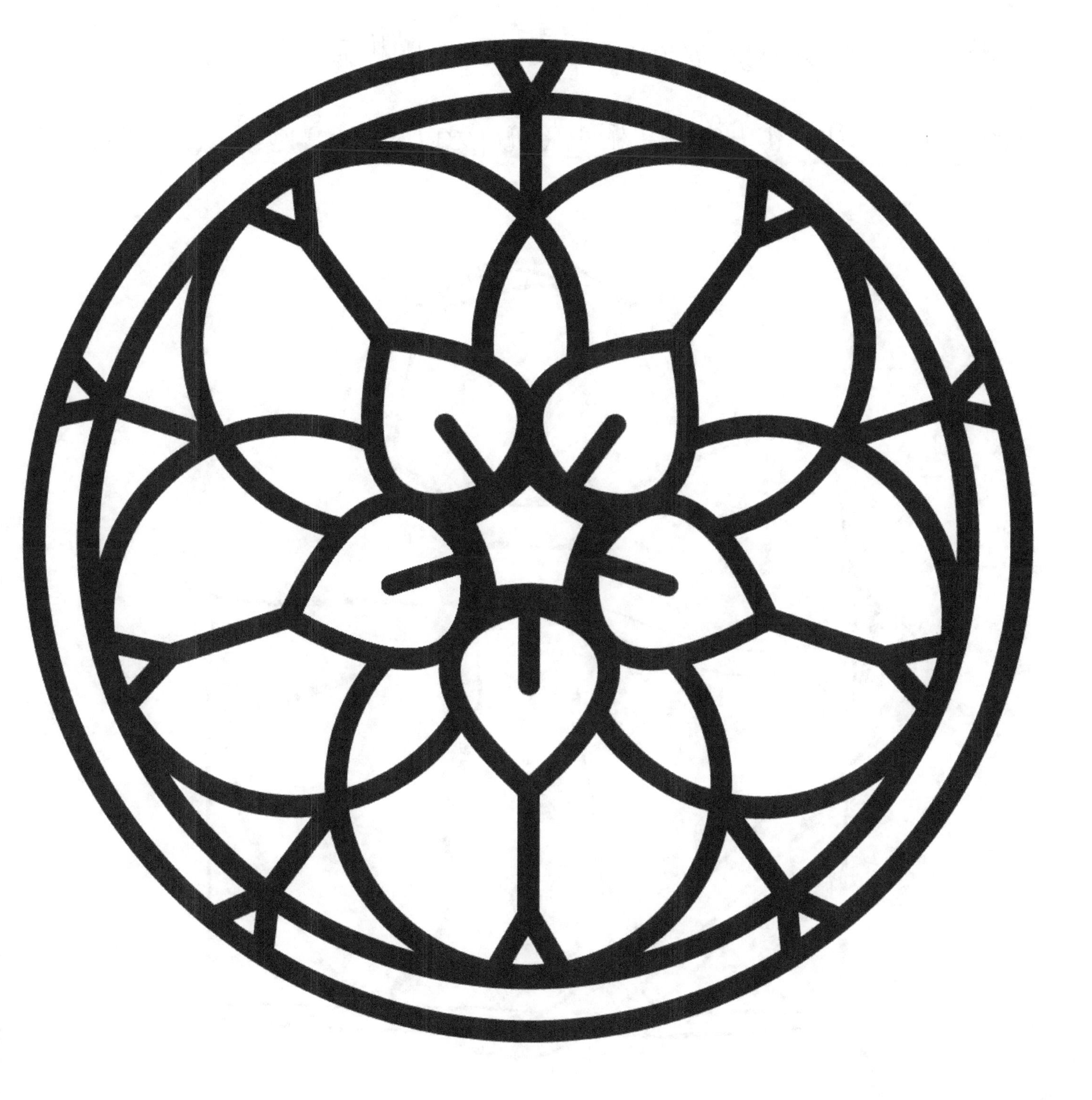

A lady wins her battles with words, but keeps a nail file in her purse, just in case.

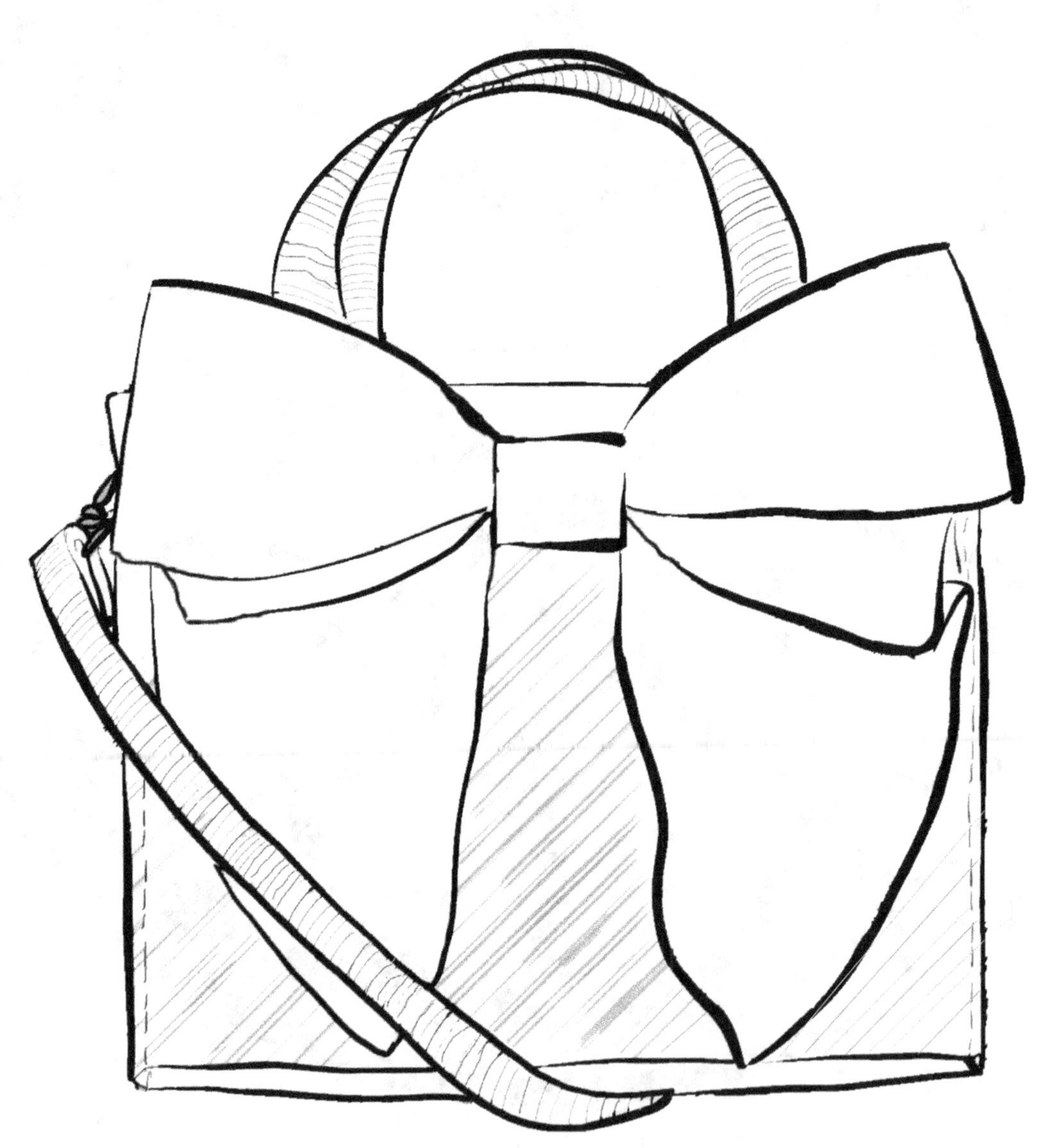

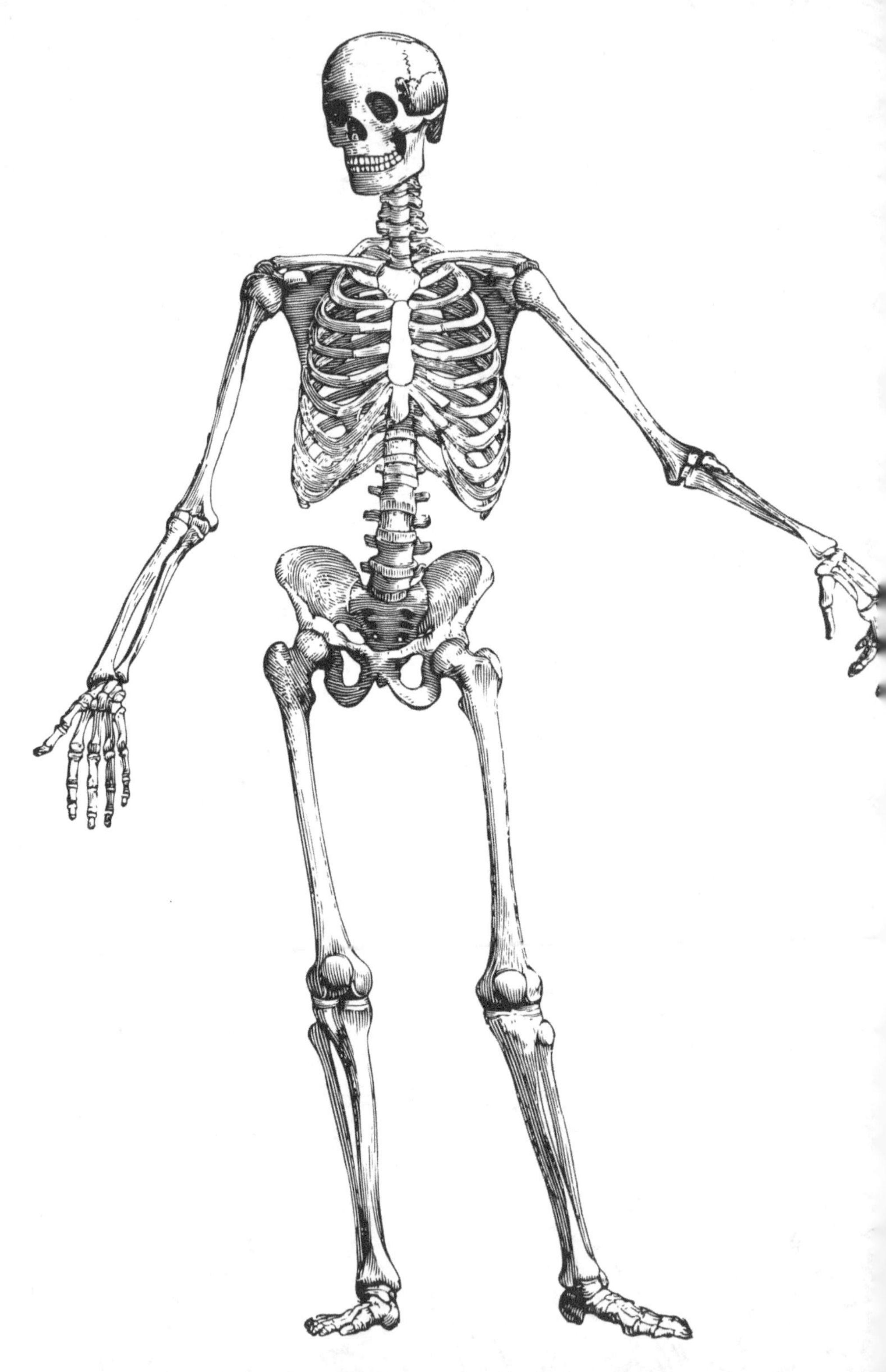

Sugar,
it's time
to give
up the
ghost.

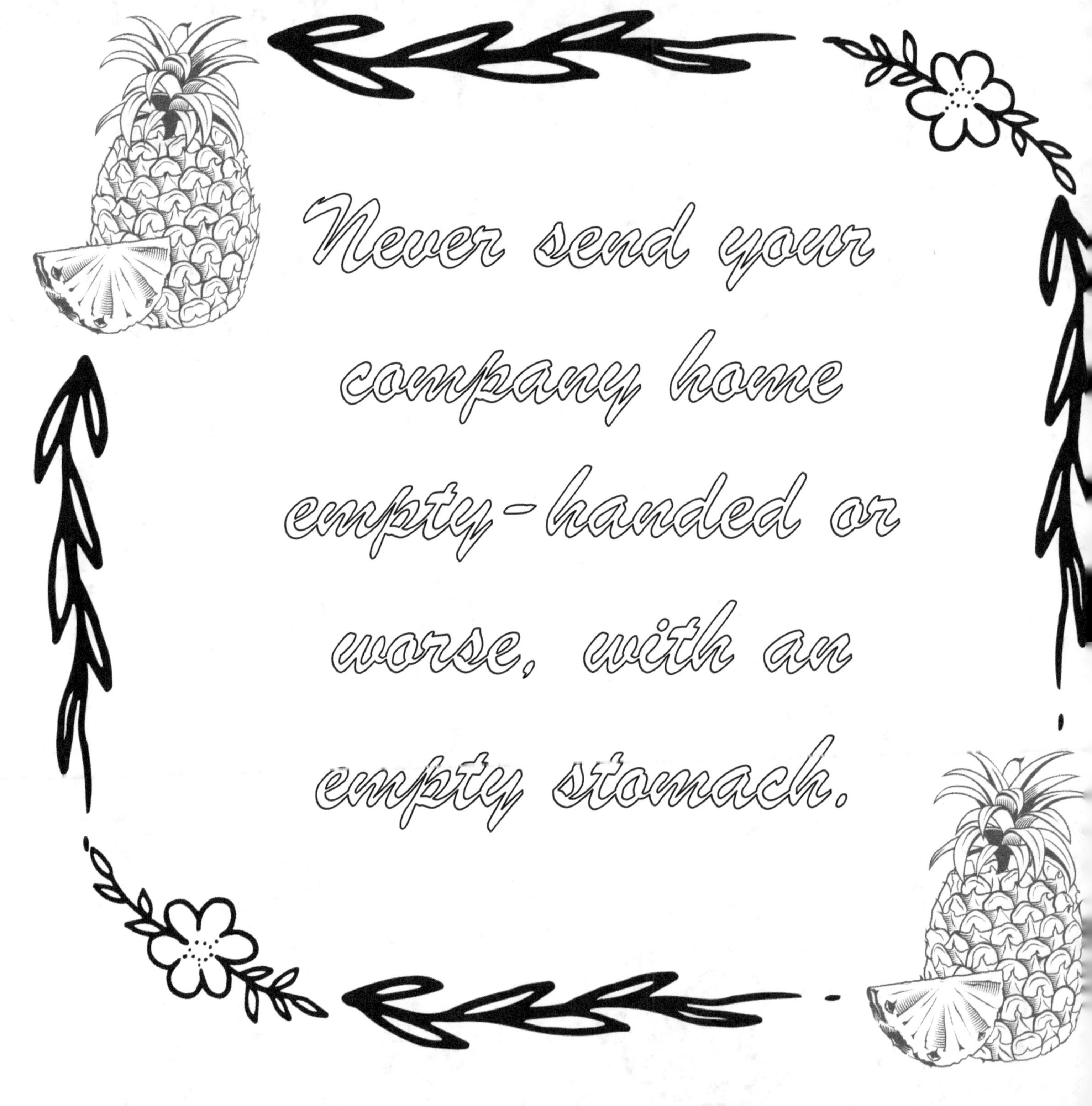
Never send your company home empty-handed or worse, with an empty stomach.

WITH LOVE